Copyright ©2006
Dunamis Publishing Co.

This book is protected under the copyright laws of the United States of America. This book may not be copied or reprinted for commercial gain or profit. Permission will be granted upon request. No part of this book may be reproduced in any form without written permission from the author or publisher. All rights reserved.

    Scripture quotations marked (NIV) are from the Holy Bible, New International Version® NIV®. Copyright 1973, 1978, 1984 by International Bible Society. All rights reserved. Scripture quotations marked (MSG) are from The Message Remix® MSG®. Scripture taken from The Message. Copyright © 1993, 1994, 1995, 1996, 2000, 2001, 2002. Used by permission of NavPress Publishing Group. Unless otherwise identified, Scripture quotations are from the King James Version of the Bible. All rights reserved.

Published by: Dunamis Publishing Co.
                P.O. Box 2375
                Ft. Campbell, KY 42223
                dunamispublishing@hotmail.com
Cover By: D. Brian Howell. ......White Dove Printing, Inc.
Printed By: White Dove Printing, Inc.
ISBN: 0-9791762-0-4

This book is based on true events however it has been made fiction to protect the characters in it.

My God, our God is all that we need for Him to be. He is the great I AM and there is no one who can do what He can do and you have to know that. God is God. The one and only, the one TRUE God, and there isn't another that can take His place.

Isaiah 43:18-19, 18 Remember ye not the former things, neither consider the things of old. 19 Behold, I will do a new thing; now it shall spring forth; shall ye not know it?

FOREWORD PAGE

The Bible says in the book of Ecclesiastes 3:1(KJV) "TO EVERYTHING there is a season, and a time to every purpose under the heaven". Keisha Lapsley's "A Woman's Dilemma" tells the story of her spiritual, physical, and psychological scars stemming from her hidden abuse as a young child growing up into a Christian woman with memories of her past. This book shows women that God can do more that what we could possibly imagine regardless of how vicious our past and present may try to determine our self worth. " Now unto Him that is able to do exceeding abundantly above all that we ask or think, according to the power that worketh in us" Ephesians 3:20. This book will not only bless you, but it will show you that "YOU CAN MAKE IT, AND ENJOY LIFE!" and that JESUS is the end state!

                               Minister Douglas L. Lapsley
                               Co-Founder
                               Dunamis Publishing Co.

A Woman's Dilemma…Keisha has written a gem of a book. She took her years of personal experiences of sexual abuse and now shares with the world how she was able to overcome these traumatic experiences through a relationship with God based on His Word. Keisha learned too early how sustained affects of childhood sexual abuse can remain and recur throughout life for women who have not healed spiritually or emotionally. She shares with us some of her survival strategies that women use to cope with childhood physical and emotional trauma-strategies that include denial, repression, depression, secrecy until she found the ultimate release that brought about the much needed healing process. Gaining strength from the Word and loving support from those close to her she was able to put into perspective the plan that God had ordained for her life…to be able to minister and speak into the lives of others that may find themselves in similar situations. (…but God meant it unto good, to bring to pass, as it is this day, to save much people alive." Genesis 50:20b). It is a blessing that she is now free to share her experiences so that others will know that they too can be free and live a life of victory.

> Bishop Harold K. Browning,
> Pastor and Founder
> Faith Mission Ministries, Inc.

DEDICATION

I give honor to God first and foremost. He is the one who got me through the hurts and the pains and healed me. He believed in me before I even knew Him and I dedicate this book to Him. Lord I thank You and praise You for all that You do for me. Also, I dedicate this book to women who have either given up or almost given up. This book is here to encourage you, to give you hope and peace in the midst of your storm.

ACKNOWLEDGEMENTS

I would like to acknowledge my husband: To my one and only, my husband Douglas Lapsley. He is truly a man of God and carries the love of God in his heart. He is a man after God's own heart. He is my biggest supporter. He has had my back from beginning to end with this book and anything that I have done or will do. Baby, you are my heart and with every heartbeat beats my love for you. I love you more than you will ever know. I desire to make mention of my children, Mar'shon, Kiante, and Christilyn Lapsley. I love you. Ya'll are momma's babies. I want to thank my Pastor and Co-Pastor Bishop Harold K. and Prophetess Gwen Browning for loving me and praying for me. You are true examples of Christ. To my parents Mark and Patsy Longino: I love you. I couldn't ask for better parents. I know that this blessing of a book will bring a smile to your faces and I know that you are rejoicing with me. I love you Taj. I wouldn't trade you for any other brother. You are a "tru" supporter of me. You always tell me to go forth and I thank you. To my mother- in- law, I love you Hilda Williams. Maurice and Landa Shingleton, I love you guys. Much love to you. I have got to give shout outs to my girl Rosa Potter (my twin). Girl you know that I love you. You are a "tru" friend and have been there through it all and always have my back. Thank you! I also have to thank Christy Kirkland because you pushed me when it was needed. Thank you. To Elder and Evangelist Caldwell thank you for help with information and Val your words of encouragement. You just don't know how your words added season to my walk in the faith. Jennifer Myrick, I love ya girl. You have supported me and rejoiced with me every time and it was a true praise, a true rejoicing.

Terry Hopkins, thank you for everything. I love you. I'd like to thank Teresa (my printer) for her encouraging words, testimonies, and her love. I love ya girl! You and your company worked very hard and helped me in so many ways and God is truly going to bless you because He knows your heart. Brian you did a beautiful job on the book cover. You sir, are anointed. Thank you. I thank everyone who encouraged me, spoke life over this book and was like girl I can't wait til your book comes out. Well ya'll it's out! Thank you Jesus!

TABLE OF CONTENTS

Poem
Salvation Page
Things that make you go hmmm…
Kenisha's Dilemma
Chapter 1
Chapter 2
Chapter 3
Kenisha's Deliverance
Chapter 4
Chapter 5
Kenisha's Freedom
Chapter 6
Chapter 7
Chapter 8
Chapter 9
Chapter 10
Let Freedom Reign in you

SHE BREAKS FREE

Even though I'm a grown woman
there is a little girl inside,
She's dying to come out and be free,
but she's afraid.
Afraid of what you ask?
Afraid of being rejected again,
Afraid of being put down again,
Afraid of not being accepted,
She's afraid of losing the little that she has gained.
So how do they keep the little girl inside?
They continue to do what they have always
done, which is:
they continue to beat her up every time she
comes out.
So she folds back up and doesn't come out.
Even though she wants to grow up and
mature she feels she can't.
They let her out sometimes cause they bless her
with material things but it's not enough.
She looks for so much more.
What does she look for you ask?
She looks for acceptance.
She looks for happiness not bittersweet.
She looks for confidence.
She wants to cry out.
And she does cry out, but no one hears her.
How does she break free?
She breaks free by the love of God!
She breaks free by the fire of God in her heart!
She breaks free in making Jesus her Savior!
She breaks free by trusting in the Lord!

She breaks free by letting God increase in her!
She breaks free by leaning on the Almighty God!
She breaks free by being intimate with God in prayer!
She breaks free by guarding her heart with all diligence; for out of it flow the issues of life! (Pro 4:23)
VICTORY! SHE HAS BROKEN FREE!

If you became saved while reading this book here is a place to celebrate your spiritual "birthday". Write it down and remember your birth always.

My Name_____

_____

My Date of Salvation_____

A Brief Description of how I felt when I gave my life to God_____

_____
_____
_____
_____
_____
_____
_____
_____
_____
_____
_____

THINGS THAT MAKE YOU GO HMMM...

What do you do when life has thrown or dealt you a bad hand?

What do you do when on the outside everyone thinks you have it made, but on the inside you are living in spiritual poverty?

What do you do when you want to cry out but you feel that no one will hear you?

What do you do when you live with so much fear that you are too scared to open your eyes in a dark room?

What do you do when you are living in such fear, looking over your shoulders every time you are waking alone, but there is no one there, except the fear that you brought with you?

What do you do when people don't understand you and the things that you do because of things done to you?

What do you do when people talk about you because they don't know the things that you've been through?

What do you do?............

Well, we as women need to know that the answers to all those questions and more is in Jesus Christ our Lord and Savior. This is what it will look like if you call on Jesus:

What do you do when life has thrown or dealt you a bad

hand and you call on Jesus?

His reply: I died for you so that you can give Me what you are carrying.

As stated in *Acts 2:21, And it shall come to pass, that whosoever call upon the name of the Lord shall be saved. (KJV)*

The dictionary says that save means to rescue someone or something from danger. Jesus Christ came to do that for us. For God so loved the world, that He gave his only begotten Son, that whosoever believeth in Him should not perish but have everlasting life, (John 3:16). He is here to snatch us up from the danger of sin. He also snatches us up from other dangers as well. You may say to yourself that well what if the danger has already happened? Physically, yes it has but the physical danger itself is gone. Now it's time to grab a hold of your spiritually. So, what does that mean? It means that you can still be saved. You can still be delivered just by calling on the name of the Lord Jesus. *Psalms 34:18 says, The Lord is nigh unto them that are of a broken heart; and saveth such as be of a contrite spirit. (KJV)* So He is not so far away that He can't hear you or feel you and you haven't done anything so bad that He can't forgive you. *Matthew 12:31 says, wherefore I say unto you,* **<u>ALL MANNER</u>** *of sin and blasphemy* **<u>SHALL BE FORGIVEN</u>**: *but the blasphemy against the Holy Ghost shall not be forgiven unto men. (KJV)* God's words said **<u>ALL MANNER OF SIN</u>** and blasphemy **<u>SHALL BE FORGIVEN.</u>** Sin is sin whether big or small. So again there is nothing that you have done that God won't forgive you for. And for those that don't know what contrite means, it's grieving and penitent for sin or shortcoming. (As was previously stated before in Psalms 34:18).

What do you do when on the outside everybody thinks that you have it made, but on the inside you live in spiritual poverty and you call on Jesus?

His reply: I died for you so that you can give Me what you are carrying.

I Corinthians 3:16 NIV says, Don't you know that you yourselves are God's temple and that Gods' Spirit lives in you? Now that we know that our body is a temple we also know that it must be furnished right? A temple is a building used for worship and to minister to the needs of people. In order to worship and minister to the needs of people then we must furnish our bodies with prayer, studying to show ourselves approved, praising God, and fasting.

Also, according to *Galatians 5:22-23* we can furnish our temples *with love, joy, peace, longsuffering, gentleness, goodness, faith, meekness, and temperance.* Also, we must do an *Ephesians 6:14-18a, Stand therefore, having our loins girt about with truth, and having on the breastplate of righteousness; and our feet shod with the preparation of the gospel of peace; above all, taking the shield of faith, wherewith ye shall be able to quench all the fiery darts of the wicked, and the helmet of salvation, and the sword of the spirit which is the word of God, and praying always with all prayer and supplication in the Spirit.* It may seem like a lot but it really isn't. Just ask God for direction. All things take time and walking in God's fullness is a process. It's not going to happen overnight. If we have declared God as I personal savior then spiritual poverty shouldn't be an issue but sometimes it happens but we are not to stay there. Life throws us punches but we are not just to **go** through but we are to **grow** through as my Pastor teaches us. He also said something when I first started going to the church, he said, "even though you failed you are **NOT** failure". I just cried because I just believed that I was a failure and to hear those words, that uplifted me so. We may mess up but it is okay as long as we repent and turn away from such things that got us into spiritual poverty in the first place. So I do know what it is like to be in Christ but be in poverty spiritually. So be encouraged, remember who you are in God, and who God is and you will make it through.

What do you do when you want to cry out but you feel that no one will hear you and you call on Jesus?
His reply: I died for you so that you can give Me what you are carrying.
(Isaiah 59:1) Surely my arm is not too short to save, nor My ear too dull to hear. If you haven't made God the Lord of your life, He says this to you, *(II Chronicles 7:14) if my people, who are called by my name, will humble themselves and pray and seek my face and turn from their wicked ways, then will I hear from heaven and will forgive their sin and will heal their land.* Call on Jesus and believe in Him and God will comfort you in an instant. It's like a parent whose child has been missing for a number of years and finally they are reunited. Their hearts are comforted and overjoyed. Recognize Him! But if you have made God the Lord of your life God says to you, just allow Me to reign in your life. Get all the benefits that I have for you. You are My child and as a Father I will take care of you if you let me.

What do you do when you live with so much fear that you are too scared to open your eyes in a dark room and you

call on Jesus?
His reply: I died for you so that you can give Me what you are carrying.
II Timothy 1:7 says, "I have not given you the spirit of fear but of power and of love and of a sound mind." Keep repeating this scripture until it gets into your spirit and until you believe it without a shadow of a doubt. Fear is the enemy's greatest tactic on people.

According to *I John 4:18, There is no fear in love. But perfect love drives out fear, because fear has to do with punishment. The one who fears is not made perfect in love.* So what this tells us is that if *we love God with all our heart, all of our soul, all of our strength, and all of our mind according to Luke 10:27,* we can overcome fear. If we are in fear then our love for God has not been perfected. To love God like He desires for us to love Him then He **HAS** to be first in our lives. **HE IS PRIORITY!** I use to be so scared and so fearful but the more I put my trust and faith in God the less I fear. I believe that I was one of the scariest people alive but once God came in and I knew in my heart that **HE IS MY PROTECTOR, MY JEHOVAH NISSI, THE LORD MY BANNER** I could sleep in peace. Let the devil who stole peace, sleep, and rest from you steal no more! Let him know the God that you serve and put him back under your feet. Be empowered with the word of God.

What do you do when you are living in such fear, looking over your shoulders every time you are walking alone, but there is no one there except the fear that you brought with you and you call on Jesus?
His reply: I died for you so that you can give Me what you are carrying.
Joshua 1:9 says, "Have I not commanded you? Be strong

and courageous. Do not be terrified; do not be discouraged, for the Lord your God will be with you wherever you go." I would be walking alone in the street in the dark and I would be so scared because of past attacks therefore, I would become paranoid. Looking over my shoulder every 3 seconds because of every noise that I would hear and I finally grew tired of it all. Fear is a state of mind. The more I thought about what was "falsely" going on around me, the more I became frantic. That let me know that all of it was in my mind because I gave my mind over to imaginations and the enemy walked right on in and played that videotape every time I let him until I got a hold of myself and gave my fear over to God. I told him that I was scared and afraid and that's when I got the scripture II Timothy 1:7 as stated above. Don't allow the enemy to use the videotape with your mind any longer. Do you know what you do with videotapes that you don't want anymore, you throw them away. Throw away the videotape and repeat II Timothy 1:7 everyday until you get it into your spirit. Plead the blood of Jesus over your mind and take back your thought process from imaginations. Imaginations are not yours until you make a home for it. Just like when you go to the store and you see a chocolate cake, it's not yours until you pay for it and take it home. Matthew 11:12 says, *"And from the days of John the Baptist until now the kingdom of heaven suffereth violence, and the violent take it by force."* We must take back our minds and profess that we have the mind of Christ daily.

What do you do when people don't understand you or the things that you do because of things done to you and you call on Jesus?

His reply: I died for you so that you can give Me what you are carrying.

Even though people may not understand you, you must *be confident of this very thing, that He (God) who has begun a good work in you shall perform it until the day of Jesus Christ (Phil 1:6).* We are all a work in progress. I heard a preacher say once; *"I have more authority than other people's opinions about me."* We cannot be controlled by other people's thoughts but what we should be concerned about is making sure that God is pleased and when He is pleased we don't have to worry about others because all things will fall in line.

What do you do when people talk about you because they don't know the things that you have been through and you call on Jesus?
His reply: I died for you so that you can give Me what you are carrying.

Always remember this, they talked about Jesus, so what makes us above our Master? Be confident in knowing that God is God and people don't have to necessarily understand what you go through as long as you give Him the praise. Praise Him for what He has brought you out of. *We have to guard our hearts with all diligence for out of it flows the issues of life according to Proverbs 4:23.*

One way we can guard our hearts is through praise. Praise Him even the more when people talk about you. Jesus was ridiculed and we have to face the fact that we will be too. God takes us through trails and tribulations so we can witness to others from our testimonies. How can we help others if we never go through anything? Don't worry about what people think of you. I know that you say, "that is easier said than done." Nevertheless, believe me when I say worrying about people will make you mentally ill and physically ill. Are you sick all the time and don't understand why? Are you at a standstill in your walk with God or in life period?

Search your heart and see if you are standing still or sick because you realize that you are more worried about what people are saying about you and what they think about you. God needs soldiers in His army and when in battle soldiers have to be in position and if they are not in position during battle then either someone else or you yourself may get killed or wounded. Soldiers don't have time to put down their weapons in the middle of a fight to stop and see what someone is saying about them. If we allow what other people say to us or about us dictate our walk with God then what good are we to His kingdom. When we do that we make people the Lord of our lives instead of God. Remember, people don't have to know what God is doing for you and what He has done for you as long as you know. What you have to know is this, the same people that are talking about you wasn't there when you was crying on the floor praying to God to help you in that situation. They weren't there when you couldn't afford to speak negative to your situation because it would cost you your deliverance. **THEY WERE NOT THERE! YOU WERE!** So don't worry about if they don't understand your praise and why you do what you do. Be confident in God and let Him do battle for you.

In this book I will tell a story from beginning to end about the act, the struggles, the deliverance, and the victory. Remember *God does not show favoritism according to Romans 2:11*, so if He did it for me He will surely do it for you. There is something that you must do first and that is to make Him Lord and Savior of our life so that you may have a complete and full deliverance. Invite Him in and ask Him to come into your heart and clean you up. God will perform His word and will do just that for you.

I am the narrator of this story. I am going to share a story with you about a woman named Kenisha. She has allowed me to share this part of her life with you. Kenisha felt that if she shared her story then maybe she could help someone. She really wanted me to convey that God is her only deliverer. It was no one else that got her to where she is now. It was God and Him alone and if you desire the same freedom then God is the only way. Kenisha said that she wants you to feel what she went through and also to take part in her victory because if you can understand and relate to what she will be sharing through her story then you to can have the victory and be free too.

KENISHA'S DILEMMA

Chapter 1
"The Baby Shower"

"Surprise!" everyone yelled. "Oh my goodness. I can't believe you all did this. Oh, I'm gonna get ya'll. Man ya'll ain't right", said Kenisha. "Gurl you know we had to do it like this. You my girl and a bag of pearls so you know it had to go down like this", said Tyenna. "Did we get cha or did we get cha"? Teasia said laughingly. Yeah ya'll got me. It's all-good though. One of ya'll gone be next. "Pssh... girl please the only one that will be carrying babies will be you now and you later", said one of the sisters from church. "Ooh that ain't cool", Kenisha said while laughing. "All right make room for the mama. Give her the big chair before she falls over", Tyenna said. "Now after I sit in this chair, I hope there is some food coming to my lap". Shemila said, "dang lil ma you always got food on tha brain but don't worry we got you a smorgasbord". "Uh uh no you didn't. Well since you did let me have a taste test", Kenisha said laughing. "Girl I have got to win my games first. I am ready", Shemila said. Everyone started laughing. The baby shower went on, they played games and they fed Kenisha. "Man this food is bangin'. Ya'll put cha foot in this", said Kenisha. "Well we are glad that you are enjoying it", Tyenna said. "All I want to know now is, where is the desert cause I know there is some banana pudding up in here", Kenisha said. "Sista, and you this. It's off tha chain too", Teasia said. "Boi, I'm gonna put a hurtin on it too", Kenisha said. "Have you thought about names for the baby", one of the church members asked? We are still not sure yet. Do you want to have a boy or girl, another one asked? Well I want a boy but I am happy with what God blesses me with. You already have two boys. Are you sure you want another one? "What about a girl", a sister asked. "Naw, I will be cool with another boy". "You right cause we can't have another one of you walking around here", a sister said jokingly. Then all the women started laughing. All the women enjoyed themselves clownin' and having a good time. Oh my, the surprise baby shower was so beautiful. Kenisha was blessed with many gifts.

    The only thing about the baby shower is that Kenisha was there physically but mentally she was scared and confused. After the baby shower was over and everyone went home it was just Tyenna and Kenisha at Tyenna's house. Now Tyenna was wondering were Kenisha was.

    "Kenisha! Kenisha! Where are you"? But Kenisha didn't answer. All of a sudden Tyenna heard some sniffling. "Key is that you? Are you all right? Why are you in the bathroom cryin'?" "I'll be fine Ty". "Obviously not Key, you are in a bathroom cryin' after your baby shower. Dog, was the baby shower that bad?" Kenisha started laughing. "That's tha Key I know and love, now what's up? Talk to ya girl." "Well Tyenna you know that I don't know if I'm having a boy or girl", Kenisha said crying." "Yeah", said Tyenna. "To tell you the truth I am scared to death of which one I will have. I guess when ol' girl asked me about a having a girl it triggered all of this", said Kenisha. "Kenisha, why don't you want to have a little you running around here", Tyenna asked? "I don't want a girl", Kenisha said in a snappy way. "Why", asked Tyenna? "Ty there's so much that you don't know", said Kenisha. "Well tell me. I don't have nothin' but time", said Tyenna.

Kenisha went on to say, "I hope you are ready for a story. Okay here it goes. It was a nice summer day and man it was hot. It was only morning time and outside already felt like 95 degrees but of course on the inside it was nice and cool because the air conditioner was on. I was about seven years old. We lived in a middle class neighborhood. The houses were so nice and all the neighborhood kids played together. We would have block parties in the neighborhood. It was the place to be. Well life to me at that time was so carefree, nothing could ever happen. Life was still so innocent for me. On this particular morning I was laying on the floor on my stomach holding my head up with my hands, chillin' watching Sesame Street. This day started like any other day. Both of my parents were at work and a lady stayed and watched me. I was dressed for the day. My mom made sure that I was taken care of before she went to work. Anyways, as I was watching Sesame Street the lady wanted to do my hair. So I sat on the couch with her and she laid out all my stuff. Man, it was like she was prepared. What trips me out, was that my mom had done my hair but she said she just wanted to do my hair". Then the lady said, "you have to sit on my lap for me to do your hair". Kenisha continued to say, "so she started to do my hair and then in an instant my life as I knew it was stripped. Everything that I knew to have understood was no longer. The simplicity of life was over. My world had switched from all that innocence to confusion, fear, and questions came rollin' in. She had touched me in my secret place. I didn't know what to think. I didn't even know how to respond. While I continued to sit in her lap she sexually pushed on me back and forth and kept rubbing on me. Nobody had ever told me (that I could remember anyway) that no one should touch me there. I was now introduced into the world of sex, and not the way that sex was intended. This sexual contact was improper in the worst way. I guess the lady went home so-called satisfied, after it was all done and over with. But for me, I was still sitting at home wondering what in the world just happened. I didn't say anything to my parents. I was told not to say anything. I wouldn't have anyway because I thought that I would get in trouble. I would see the lady once in a while and when we were around other people she would call me nasty and make me feel lower than dirt. She actually called me nasty and my feelings were so hurt. I was embarrassed and didn't know how to come back from that. I would walk around with my head down. Now the molestation didn't happen all the time because my parents were there but the times they weren't it was understood and it became normal for me. It may not have happened a lot but once is enough for any child in any case". "No doubt. It never should have happened at all, but Kenisha what does that have to do with you not wanting to have a girl", Tyenna asked? "It's just like I told my husband. I don't want her to go through what I went through", Kenisha said. "Yeah that's what the world says but we know that our God says different. You can overcome anything", Tyenna said. "Yeah David said the same thing when I talked to him about it. He said for me to talk to his mom. You know that my mother-in-law works with abusive children", Kenisha said. "Yeah, you told me something like that", said Tyenna. "Well anyway I told him that I didn't feel comfortable talking to her about it. David is very understanding though", Kenisha said. "Well, I believe God for your deliverance. I know that God can do it and you are going to have to believe it for yourself. Don't miss out on the joys of having a little girl because of fear. I love and enjoy my daughter. I wouldn't give her away for anything in the world. Arie is my joy", Tyenna said. "I know Ty but that fear will always be there. I try not to even think that way but it just scares me sometimes. Ty, after those encounters no one could understand why I did the things that I did", Kenisha said. "Like what Key", Tyenna asked?

"Well one night I was watching television in my mom's room with her. I was lying on her bed and started touching myself. Then she yelled at me and said you don't do that. Where did you get that from and I said I don't know, but would I dare tell her, of course not. You know a child only do what is taught to them or what they see. Remember, like I said before, this became normal from me. Even as I grew older it didn't only come from that lady but other people as well. You would have thought that I had abuse me written on my forehead. It's embarrassing and humiliating. You know that people can be so judgmental and they just don't have a clue of what has happened in someone's life. I would just have to trust God and lean on Him, I guess", said Kenisha.

"Come on Kenisha let's get some fresh air", Tyenna said. "That sounds cool. I'm wit that", said Kenisha. "Thanks for listening to me and not judging me and encouraging me Ty", Kenisha said. "You know you are my gurl... I got cha back". "Where you wanna go", asked Kenisha. "It's your day, you pick", Tyenna said. "Let's go get our feet and nails done", Kenisha suggested. "That sounds good to me", Tyenna said. "Let me ask David to see if he minds", said Kenisha. "Now you know I've got to ask Ricky too", said Tyenna. Kenisha called David on her cell phone and said, "Hey babe, do you mind if I go to get my nails and feet done with Ty", Kenisha asked? "Yeah Kenisha that's cool. Finish enjoying your day man", David responded. "Thanks babe. See you when I get home then. I love you. Bye", said Kenisha. "I love you too Kenisha, Bye", said David. "All right Ty what did Ricky say", said Kenisha? "You know he was clownin", Tyenna said. "What girl, what did he say", Kenisha asked. "He was like it's about time you took care of them toe crow nails", Tyenna said. "Ty, he is so crazy", Kenisha said. As they both laughed, they drove off in Tyenna's Hummer bumpin' their Gospel hip-hop.

Chapter 2
"The Long Drive"

"You wanna go to Jonya's to get our nails and feet done", Kenisha asked? "Yeah Key, that will be cool", Tyenna said. "She does a real good job", said Kenisha. "Man, I'm ready to soak my toes", Tyenna said. "Girl, you know", said Kenisha. "Where does Jonya work", asked Tyenna? "Oh she owns Caress Beauty Spa. You know the one on Valdimir Dr.", Kenisha said. "Oh, Okay. I didn't know that she owned that spa", Tyenna said surprisingly. "Yeah, she has had it opened for about 5 months now", said Kenisha. "Shut up! Man, that's awesome", said Tyenna. "Oooh, turn that up Ty. That's my song", Kenisha yelled! "And you know this", Tyenna said. They both begin to sing the song; praising Him is important to me. I have to praise Him for what He has caused me to be. Praise Him! Praise Him! The music was bumpin'. "Jesus! I love this song", Kenisha said.

"I know, right. This song just really ministers. Key have you really listened to the words of this song", asked Tyenna? "Yeah, why do you ask me that", asked Kenisha? Because God wants you to praise Him and He has caused you to come to this place so that He can minister to you. He is bringing you to a new place in Him and He wants you to recognize some things that is going on in your life so that you can get it straight, be delivered, and move on", Tyenna said. "Only God knows that everything that I blocked out from years past is starting to reveal itself now and I just don't know what to do", Kenisha said. "Well Key, if God is starting to reveal the past to you it is for you to deal with so that it can no longer have a hold over you. In order for you to go forth in God you are going to have to deal with the issues from your past. If you don't deal with those past issues it will affect your future. Remember that because it so true. Have you noticed how you act towards people or being in relationships with the trust issues you have", Tyenna asked? "Yeah, I do", Kenisha answered. "Do you know why you react in that manner", asked Tyenna? "Not really, I just don't trust people, and why should I", said Kenisha. "It's because of your past and the things that has happened to you, so now the time has come for you to deal with these things so that you may be set free from these issues", Tyenna said. "Look Ty I hear you, I really do, but my friend I haven't even told you all of it", said Kenisha. "You mean to tell me there is more", Tyenna said. "Yes it is. I've been through a lot Ty. Let me finish telling you the rest.

Well it was the end of summer and I was excited because school was beginning. I was in the second grade. It is the first day of school and my hair was pressed. I felt so pretty. School was fun to me because I got to see my friends that I hadn't seen it months. Well after about a month after school had begun, 2 males approached me in my class. They were talking to me about my body. Yes, I said SECOND grade", Kenisha said! "Jesus, you are kidding Key", Tyenna said. "Nope-2nd grade, like I said. Their names were Tre and Montrell and they were some nasty lil' boys. It makes you wonder where they got this stuff from. They would feel on me daily. Everyday something was going on. It was a new day, but it was the same stuff. I would tell them to stop. One day it was recess and we were playing hid-n-seek, which turned into personal pleasure for them. The teacher wasn't paying attention. She hardly ever paid attention. I really don't know how she received a paycheck. Anyways, I was hiding by the woods and Montrell found me. Then he yelled for Tre and then he came over to him. Then Montrell and Tre dragged me into the woods and started to do unseemly things to me. I kept saying stop and fighting back and they finally backed off. I stayed quiet about it for a while but day-by-day more issues occurred. One day the class was coming in from recess and I was at the end of the line, well Montrell and Tre came to the back of the line (while the teacher was at the front) and they snatched me behind the wall and Montrell was in the front of me while Tre was in the back of me. I fought back as best as I could. It was like they planned this because no one was ever around. Well I finally became fed up and told my teacher Ms. Mane what was going on, but Ms. Mane didn't believe me and so she never did anything about it. So as the school year went on so did these problems, I had came home from school one day and told my mom what those boys were doing to me. My mom was on Fahrenheit. She asked me had I told the teacher and I told her yes. My mom asked me what did she do and I said nothing. So then my mom wrote a letter to Ms. Mane concerning the problem. So I came to school and handed Ms. Mane the note and said, Ms. Mane here is a note from my mom", Kenisha said. Ms. Mane said, "thank you Kenisha". "After that I went and sat down at my desk. Ms. Mane read the letter and called me up to the desk and asked me about the note", said Kenisha. She said, "Kenisha who are the two boys that are touching you"? "I told her Tre and Montrell and then I said I told you that before", said Kenisha. Then she told me to, "go back to my seat". "Then she called them outside in the hallway. I never knew what was said, but one thing I did know is that nothing changed. Now that I am an adult the only conclusion that I can come to is that she asked, they denied it, and the end result was that nothing was done. You wanna know how the obscene acts ended", Tyenna asked? "How", Tyenna asked. "Well one day, it was the beginning of the school day. We couldn't have been at school an hour. In any event, Ms. Mane left us in the room by ourselves and said that she would be right back. Opportunity knocked and boy did they open the door. Well Montrell had backed my friend up against the coat hangers and started to rip open her blouse and she kept saying stop, but you know they didn't. Everybody was laughing and she was screaming. I stood back cause I knew if I would have stepped in I would have been next and I had enough. I am sorry but we weren't tight like that for me to get involved. It ain't like anything was going to be done about it. Well Ms. Mane walked in and caught the whole thing. I can't believe that's what it took before anything was done. Is it any wonder why children don't speak up sometimes? Here I was a child that spoke up and nothing was done and basically made out of a liar. From then on I never spoke of any incident again because I didn't feel like anything would be done. Can you imagine how it feels to express and tell someone what is going on with you and people would just look the other way? Why would it take something so drastic before issues are being taken care of? You know what I'm sayin", asked Kenisha?

"Yeah, I feel you. We as adults, parents, teachers, authority figures, and etc. need to lend a listening ear unto children when they speak. I know that if my kids told me something like that I would be like your mom, on fire and I would give those boys and their parents someone to rock with and that teacher, boi would I tell her something good and I would have her job. Man that is why it is so important to have God in our lives so that we will be sensitive when dealing with children and their situations. A child should not suffer because adults don't wish to take the time to listen to them. If we don't want our children running to their peers and talking to them about adult situations and getting undeveloped answers then we as adults have to do better", Tyenna responded. "Boy, Ty you said a mouthful", Kenisha said. "Man, because that makes me so upset. I don't like to see or hear children going through things like that", Tyenna said. "Tru dat. I feel you. So, when I seen how carelessly this was dealt with I felt like it must have been my fault. I thought that I must not have done something right or either I had done something wrong. You know Ty, **small things affects a child, so imagine how big they shape a child.** Ty make this left and we are there. I'll finish telling you the rest of it later. I just want our minds to be free while we are relaxing", said Kenisha. "That sounds like a plan to me Kenisha", said Tyenna.

"Hey Jonya, what's up", Kenisha and Tyenna said at the same time? "Nothing much, what's up with ya'll", Jonya responded. "Girl we are here to get our nails and feet done", Kenisha said. "Well you know ya'll come to the right place", Jonya said. "And we know this", Tyenna and Kenisha said. "Jonya girl, your place is nice. This is cool", Tyenna said. "Thank you Tyenna. Hey Kenisha I am sorry that I couldn't make it to the baby shower but you see where I have been. I have been busy in this shop all day", Jonya said. "You straight Jonya. I understand", Kenisha said. "So how was the baby shower", asked Jonya? "Oh Jonya, it was beautiful and you know we was clownin'. I owe them for surprising me though. That was not even cool. There will be a time and a place for some serious payback. You know the more that I think about it Jonya, you was in on it too", said Kenisha. "What, who me",

Jonya said sarcastically? "What who me, yes you sista", Kenisha responded back to her with the same sarcasm. "Gurrrl, I wouldn't even worry about Kenisha. We got her good", Tyenna said.

    The women just sat and laughed about the surprise baby shower. They had a good time at the spa. They were so relaxed. Kenisha relaxed her mind and let go. She just allowed the Spirit of God to minister to her mind, soul, and body. This was a time for relaxation for her. Kenisha needed this. There is so much in her heart that just releasing a little bit felt as if a couple of loads of bricks was lifted off her shoulders.

    Can you imagine how she feels? Do you know what it is like to hold everything in for years at a time? Then on top of what you are already holding on to more situations are piling up on you. Can you only imagine? Think of it like this: You are going shopping. You stop at a few stores and buy a lot of clothes or things but you still have the whole mall to go through. You have 2 bags on one arm and 1 bag on another. You stop at some more stores and now you have 2 more bags. You don't have that same pep in your step because you are loaded down with things. Now you are looking for a stroller or something to hold all them bags but the mall is out. You still haven't been around the whole mall yet. Just imagine we are like that spiritually in a lot of ways. We walk around with baggage (heavy baggage) and don't take the time to put them down and give it to God. We need to do as Kenisha and Tyenna did and go into a spa and be pampered. In the spiritual realm that's what we need to do. We should go and talk, pray, or communicate with our Lord and Savior. Get a release, so that our God can pamper us, by letting us cry out to Him and give Him what we are carrying because He doesn't mind carrying our baggage.

Prayer is a giving of ourselves. We give Jesus all of us and present our bodies as a living sacrifice and give Him all of our cares and worries. Once we give Him all of us, He fills us up with Him. That's the best thing that we can do. Think of our Lord as a bellhop (but we know that He is more than that, Amen). A bellhop is at your service to take care of what we need. They take our baggage so that we don't have to lug it around. God does the same thing.

The ladies are in their car heading home now. "Awwwwhhh, I feel so good", Tyenna said. "You know Ty. Man I could do this about every weekend", said Kenisha. "I feel wonderful. I needed this like an addict needs a fix", said Tyenna. "Girl you are so crazy. You know you ain't right", said Kenisha. "So you feel better than, uh", asked Tyenna?

"You know Ty, yes I do. I needed to share that cause other than my husband you were the only other person that I told, other than God of course. I needed to release that. Girl, I have just begun the story", Kenisha said. "What else happened? I would think that was enough", said Tyenna. "Please, when I tell you that I have been through some stuff that is exactly what I mean", said Kenisha. "Well what else then", asked Tyenna? "Well after that school was hard for me. I was really a good girl but in bad situations. I had them fair-weather friends. I seemed to be rejected at every hand. I hardly know what if feels like to be accepted. I just kind of followed the crowd. When people wanted me around then I would go. Sometimes I was secluded. Nobody wanted to be around me. I have been surrounded by negativity all my life. What is it like to be positive? Someone needed to share that with me cause I didn't know. I didn't understand how come I was enduring such hardship. I have always felt by myself. Nobody liked me. Well let me not say anybody. I had some friends. It wasn't many though. Growing up I could count on one hand my "true friends", even up through high school. My mom will tell you today that everybody liked me and that I was well liked but that wasn't necessarily true. She didn't know the things I was going through because I didn't tell her. I had to fight classmates just to get approval. I was so fragile about anything that was said to me and it would send me into tears. My parents couldn't even understand it. They didn't know why I cared so much for what people thought of me. Man after so much rejection you are looking to be accepted from just about anybody. It ain't no secret that I am small and always have been and so I had to fight to prove something to someone else. Half the time my bark was louder than my bite. It seemed like everyday was a struggle. The "fairweather's" would talk about me and put me in the midst of situations that I had nothing to do with. It was so funny because people would act like they were my friends when my parents would come to the school and volunteer. They would want to eat with my parents and me. I mean they would stick to me like a roach on sugar. I still don't know what I did to be treated so badly. I would sit and think to myself, man there must be something wrong with me. So I would fantasize about being someone else or maybe daydream about being related to someone that was famous just to be liked. Mentally I was messed up. I was jacked up.

    So anyway, when I moved to another state, I was about 12. I was around my mom's side of the family then and it was cool. I liked the difference because I felt like this could be a new start for me. You know, nobody knows me here but my family. Maybe, just maybe, I could make some real friends. Maybe, just maybe, I will no longer have to fantasize about being someone else. But you know what I learned, you can change locations but if you don't take care of the inside meaning your heart, you will still go through the same things", said Kenisha. "You know that is true", said Tyenna. "Yeah, and that is a fact and that is hard to learn as a child. I really didn't feel like I had anyone that I could talk to and be myself with. Everything was a front. You talk about somebody with some low self-esteem. I had dealt with it for a long time. You know the spirit of low self-esteem will tell you that you aren't good enough, that someone is always better than you, and you will never measure up. It will also tell you to change who you are. The spirit of low self-esteem will always have you comparing yourself to someone else. It took me a long time to realize that I had low self-esteem and now I have to get delivered from it. Low self-esteem will dictate your every move. The spirit of low self-esteem is a serious and crafty one. Low self-esteem will even guide you to suicide if you don't handle it. I would walk around with my head down and I wouldn't be able to look people in their eyes. I am still having a time with that.

But anyway after we had been there for a while I had been at 2 schools by that time. I met some people and it was not the crowd that I shouldn't have been with, but they accepted me, to a point. Any acceptance was better than none at all. Acceptance is all I needed. So I conformed to what they did and how they were. I had never been suspended before for cussing out a teacher but it ended up that I did. Well one day, I knew that my brother and I should not have had people in the house while my parents were out but we did anyway. We let one of the boys that I knew from school in the house. I had to be about 13. Well he said that he came over for my brother but he really came over for me but I didn't realize that until later. We all were playing and I went in my room and he came in after me and we started play fighting and then he laid me down on my bed and got on top of me. I told him to get off of me but he wouldn't. He kept holding down my arms. I was kicking for him to get off of me but he was still holding me down. I screamed for my brother. My brother came in with my parent's bedpost and told him to get off me. So he did and we told him to leave the house but my dad came home. So we were busy trying to sneak him out the house. You talk about a scared sista. I was scurred, not scared but scurred. I didn't think that he would try anything like that, especially with my brother being there. I guess that he didn't think my brother would do anything because he was younger than me and smaller than me. Shoot, I was the one always protecting him. And then check this out, when I went to college he was there and not only that but he lived in my same dorm. He told one of my friends one day that I was looking good and I better watch my back. I was like yeah well he can try it but at that time I was dating David and I knew that he would look out for me.

  Well anyway, that passed. Then at home there were good days and bad days, as you know it always is when it comes to teenagers and their parents. Sometimes parents don't understand their children and the children don't understand their parents and that's where the struggle lies. I was always being compared to a friend of mine. Some of the methods they used they called reverse psychology. I believe that reverse psychology is just not sound. All it is negativity and I really don't see how anyone with issues already can prosper from that. I had enough negativity coming from people outside the house and the last thing I really needed was to be compared to someone else thinking that it would have an effect on me. The bible says that it is unwise to compare. I also heard a preacher on television one day and he said *to compare is to belittle* and I never looked at it like that but it is the truth. When you compare, somebody is going to get the short end of the stick because you are going to lift someone higher than the other. So that's what they were doing with me when they would say things like, why can't you be more like Maria. She works hard to get her A's why can't you. Do you see that", Kenisha said? "Yeah Kenisha, I do", Tyenna said. "I had never seen comparison like that before. But my parents were at their ropes end though cause they seen the good grades that I used to get I wasn't getting anymore. They had seen that I really didn't have any gumption about myself. I wasn't as outgoing as I was when I was a younger child. My parents believed in me and they knew that if I just put forth the effort, I could be whatever I wanted to be. I just didn't know it for myself. The only way that would have worked is if I had believed in myself. They tried everything and did the best that they could. Yet, I think it would have been much easier for them to ask me what was wrong or what have I went through or has something happened to you that you would like to tell us about. Instead of getting to the root of the problem they tried to deal with it or give a solution, without knowing the cause and the way that things were going I probably wouldn't have told them anyway. You and I both know that giving a solution to a problem without knowing the root isn't possible and will not be successful. Now don't get me wrong they encouraged me too. They would tell me that they were proud of me but I believe with all that I was dealing with outside the home, the negativity out weighed the rest. I have some awesome parents but some of their methods I didn't agree with like I am sure that they don't agree with my methods now that I have children. I could be a little butt head myself sometimes and I needed to be dealt with. That I can agree with. I loved to be around my family. I enjoyed being with my family.

Then when I got to high school, I really started to get some attention. That's all I needed. Boys were noticing me. I didn't think that much of myself. Who would notice me? Here is this girl with all these problems. I just blocked out a lot of things that happened in the past. No one would know who I was and what I had went through. Nobody! And I declared that no one was going to know. I put Kenisha, the sweet little girl with the problems on the back burner and I presented Kenisha the girl with attitude, and didn't care at all about anything. I really could have cared less about what anyone would say about me at that point. I would say that I didn't care or I would retaliate and became who everybody wanted me to be. I would drink alcohol, smoke weed, and lay down with them boys just to be accepted and because it was the "it" thing to do. If you wasn't doin' it then you wasn't down. I think that "laying down" was the easiest part because that's all I figured that they wanted from me. I could do that because it had been happening to me as far back as I could remember. I didn't know it then but I know it now that wasn't the way to become popular or to be liked. When you do things for other people and to please everybody else no one really thinks high of you anyway. They treat you like you treat yourself, which is like crap. If I could tell any teenager in this day and age, I would tell them to find their own self-worth and be happy with themselves. Don't worry about popularity because it's not worth all the heartache and personal drama that you put yourself through. That was who I was and the interesting thing about it is in the daytime that was me but when night time fell I still had to go to bed with myself. No one knew how many times I feel asleep crying about not liking myself and not being happy. I am 24 years old and only now; I am just knowing what it is to be truly happy, in Christ. Now I can go to sleep in peace and not in turmoil. Man you gone trip. Let me tell you this. I remember one-day things just got so bad. I had an argument with my mom and some other stuff happened at school and I just grew tired of it all and I really believed that it would be better for everybody if I weren't here. Maybe that would just make everyone's life better. I also thought if I would kill myself that I would make everyone else hurt like I was hurting. I wanted to get back at them. Now, when I think about it though that was stupid because they didn't like me anyway so they would not have even cared. In any event, I went down in the kitchen and got the sharpest knife in the house and I took it upstairs to my room. I remember closing my door and turning on my music. I sat on my bed as I looked at the knife on my dresser. I cried and cried and cried some more. I couldn't stop the tears from falling. I couldn't understand what I did to deserve all of this heartache and pain. Nothing ever seemed to work out for me. I was fighting on every hand at every turn. The only thing that stopped me from killing myself was that I didn't like pain and I knew that it would hurt", said Kenisha. "Girl, now that is pitiful", Tyenna said while laughing. "I know. I was pitiful all the way around huh but you know that sista girl don't like pain at all", Kenisha said. "It's funny because here is somebody who wants to commit suicide but is scared of the pain. I mean it is a good thing though because you are still here but that is kinda funny", Tyenna responded. "Alright, stop laughing at me", Kenisha said while laughing. "So this is what I did, I put it up in my drawer until I gathered enough courage to do it but I guess you see that I never found that courage cause I am still here. Then I grabbed my bible that my parents had given me and started to read it but I put it back up because I couldn't understand it. The knife stayed in my drawer for months.

    It bugs me sometimes when people say that suicide is a white person thing cause black people don't do that. That is not necessarily true because it has crossed my mind more than once. Suicide doesn't have a color. Suicide is something that people THINK is a solution to a problem but it is not because the problem is still not fixed and if you take your life it will never be fixed and you won't be able to be that ONE person that makes a difference in someone else's life. I didn't know it then but God wants us to make it through so that we can help someone else through their troubles. That tells me that our lives ARE valuable. Our lives mean something", Kenisha said. "Key that is somethin' serious. I had no clue", said Tyenna. "Ty, no one has", said Kenisha. "I just would have never guessed that. You have held up pretty good", said Tyenna. "You know why Ty, because I have been able to show people another face for years and so now it is the norm. I didn't know anything else. I wore a mask for years to cover up all the rejection, hurts, and pains. I even had a mask when I first met David in college. I am still unmasking myself and I am glad that he loves me more each time I unmask another part of me.

    A lot of us have masks because we are fearful to be ourselves. We don't want to be rejected but rejection is going to happen whether we like it or not because there is always going to be someone that doesn't like something that you do or don't do. It's time for God's people to do an unmasking and to know what it is to be truly happy. I know that it was all a plan from the beginning. The enemy knew what God had in store for me. Therefore, if he could send me down another pathway then he was going to do it. I have found out that it is a choice that we make what path we follow. I do know that I have to stop conforming to what people want me to be because I am missing out on who God wants me to be and what God has for me. It is something that I am still learning though because now I know God and I know that He has something better for me. It is for me to go out and to help someone else", Kenisha said. "As our pastor says all the time, we are not only to go through but also to grow through, so that we can help someone else. Have you talked to Pastor about any of this", Tyenna said? "No, as I stated before, you and David are the only ones that know", Kenisha said. "You know that is what your Pastor is there for. He is there to help you", said Tyenna in a voice of concern. "Okay, you know, I hear what you are saying, but the fact still remains that I am scared of rejection. What if he or co-pastor doesn't look at me the same? What then", Kenisha asked inquisitively? "Kenisha understand this, God has placed pastor and co-pastor as our Shepard's and He has equipped them to handle all sorts of issues. They come into contact with people all the time and I am sure that you are not the first one that they have dealt with concerning these types of issues. Their service is not to judge but to counsel and I believe that they will do just that. We have awesome pastors and they pastor with much integrity", said Tyenna. "So, do you think that I really should talk to Pastor and Co-Pastor Rural", asked Kenisha? "Yes I do. Get some counseling so that you can get on your road to recovery", said Tyenna. "Recovery, man you sound like Doctor M.D.", Kenisha said jokingly. "I sure appreciate you listening to me though. Let me call David to see if he is still at your house", Kenisha said. "You know he probably is", Tyenna said. "Hey babe, where are you at", Kenisha said to David as she was talking to him on her cell phone. "I'm still over here with Ricky. How did everything go", asked David? "Awwwwhhh man, it was nice. I feel so good", Kenisha said. "Well it's time for you to come on home now", David said. "I know", said Kenisha. "I am tired anyway. I am ready to come home. What are the kids doing", Kenisha asked? "They are playing with Nick and you know they are battling each other on the playstation", David said. "Well I hope they know that they are going to lay it down when we get home", Kenisha said. "No doubt", said David. "We got to get up early for church in the morning, so when we get home, it's all over", David said yawning. "Don't be yawnin' cause you makin' me yawn", Kenisha said. "You know that this baby needs rest and if I don't get rest, the baby will toss and turn all night. Well I am getting ready to get off the phone cause we are almost at the house", said Kenisha. All right then Babe; I will see you when you get here", David said as they both hung up the phone. "What are they doin' at the house", Tyenna said. "Well the kids are playing on the playstation and the men are just layin' in tha cut", Kenisha said. "What are you wearing to church tomorrow", Tyenna said? "I think I am going to wear a cruise ship", Kenisha said. "Oh no you didn't", Tyenna screamed laughing. "Shoot, girl you know what my wardrobe is like since the baby. I call my clothes just what they are which is ships and buses cause that's just how big those clothes are", Kenisha said. "You need to stop", Tyenna said while laughing. "What do you mean", Kenisha said to her sarcastically. "Well then at least what color will you be wearing", Tyenna said. "Um, let me see, a cruise ship is white and a bus is yellow. Iny miny miney moe, the color yellow is bright so it has gots to go. I pick white", Kenisha said. Tyenna just laughed and said, "all right then". "What are you wearing tomorrow", Kenisha asked? "I don't know yet. I will probably wear my pen-stripe pants suit. That's if I don't find anything else", said Tyenna. Thanks again for everything Ty, the baby shower and all. Everything was just beautiful", Kenisha said. "You are welcome. You know that you are my girl and I got'cha back. You know I couldn't let bring a baby into this world and not give you a baby shower. Now come on this is me you are talking about", Tyenna said. As they pulled up in Tyenna's driveway, they seen their husband's standing outside talking.

Chapter 3
"Coming into Realization"

"What ya'll doin' out here", Tyenna asked? "What you doin' out here", David jokingly responded. " You know what, don't you start with me", said Tyenna, while she laughed. "Ya'll are forever going at it", Kenisha said. Ricky said, "Well what did it look like we was doing when ya'll pulled up?" " You know what brotha, you better zip it, cause you gotta stay home with me and if you don't want to be on the street then you better catch the hiccups from trying to stop laughing, Tyenna said jokingly. "Oooh... Ricky you know there is no room for you at our house dude. We'd like to help you but we can't. Sorry", Kenisha said while laughing! "Ricky man, I got'cha back", David said. "Oh, do you now David", Kenisha said. "Woman! I'm tha man of tha house and you will submit", said David. Everyone busted out laughing. Then David said, "Baby I'm sorry, I'm sorry, I'm sorry". "Naw brotha, but you will be", Kenisha said while cutting her eyes at him. "Kenisha, I wouldn't take that", Tyenna said. "Gurrrl you know I got ALL of this under control", Kenisha said. "Tyenna, you stay out of it before I have to put tha smack down on you", said Ricky. "No, he didn't. Kenisha, you and David are going to have to go because I need to check this man", said Tyenna. " Ya'll are off tha chain for real", Kenisha said. "We are going to get out of here so we will get up with ya'll later", David said. "Cool. We will see ya'll tomorrow then", Rick said. "Send Jabreel and Deon to the truck", Kenisha said. "Hey boys did ya'll have fun", Kenisha asked them. "Yes ma'am", Jabreel and Deon both answered. "Come on and get in the truck", David said.

"Man Sweet, you have a lot of gifts from the baby

shower. It took forever to pack up the truck. It took so long the boys are sleep already. Look at them in the back seat. They are laid out ain't they", David said. "Yeah, they are gone. Boy that was quick", Kenisha said. "Yeah well we ain't going to have to worry about them playing when we get home. They are going to go straight to bed. Did you have a good time at the spa", David asked? "It was nice both physically and spiritually", Kenisha said. "Why, what did ya'll talk about", David asked? "You know, what you and I have talked about before, about my past and the things that I went through and dealt with", Kenisha responded. "Oh, okay. What did Tyenna say", David asked? "She really just listened and threw in some suggestions for me to think about. She also suggested that I talk to our pastors about it and the effects that it had on me, so that I can grab a hold of my deliverance", said Kenisha. "How do you feel about what she said", David asked? "Well, you know, I heard what she said but I just don't think that I am ready to talk to our pastors or anyone for that matter about the whole thing. Man do you know what it took just to tell you and her", Kenisha said. "But maybe there is something to what she said. I want you to be delivered and I know you want to be delivered too. God can only help you when you help yourself and you don't have to do much but just ask for His help", David said. "Yeah, well I can get delivered without having to tell everyone", Kenisha said as she snapped at him. "But, you will need guidance", David said in a firm voice. "Well then it would seem that I am at a crossroad, uh", Kenisha said. "Don't get offended babe, I just want to help", David said. I'm not offended; I just want to be able to handle things in my own way and at this point I am tired of talking about it", Kenisha said. "You ought to be able to see that your way isn't working and your way is keeping you at a standstill. Look I love you Kenisha and I just want you to live and have life and have it more abundantly as the bible says. That's why Jesus came. He wants you to be free", David said. "I hear what you sayin", Kenisha said. "No, but are you adhering", David said. "Like I said I hear what you sayin", Kenisha said? "Sweet don't be upset. I'm saying this as soft as I can and I ain't gone take too much of you talking to me like that", said David. "I know that you are and I appreciate that but you are my husband and it took years for me to tell you, so don't you think it would be harder for me to tell other people", Kenisha said. "What you have to understand is that pastors are not just other people, but they have been chosen, appointed by God to lead and guide God's people and our pastors have been appointed over us", David said. "Some of these things are embarrassing, humiliating, and shameful David", Kenisha said. "How do you figure that? Because, it would seem to me that the situations that have taken place in your life like molestation and attempted rape, and so on and so forth are things beyond your control. Remember when you told me, that when you was in school you was dating some dude and ya'll was out walking one night and then ya'll stood behind a building and he pushed you up against the wall and started feeling on you and touching you and forcing himself on and you kept saying stop and he wouldn't. Then he put your arms up on the wall and you kept saying stop but he wouldn't. Do you remember that", David asked? "Yeah, I do", Kenisha said. "Well how do you figure that it is humiliating, shameful, and embarrassing", David asked? "Do you really want to know why? Do you really want to know", Kenisha asked David boldly? "Yeah, I really want to know", David said in the same response. "I feel that way because, I shouldn't have put myself in that position.

You know when that date happened all I could think about is maybe I should not have been walking outside with him at night or maybe I should not have been so naive. I also kept dating him after that. I was numb to it all. He called me out my name a few times but I still didn't leave. The thing that is most surprising is that I really didn't like him but because I was numb to it all. I stayed because I didn't know what it meant to be in a good relationship. That is shameful no matter how you look at it. Many times people wonder how come women stay when they are treated so badly and it is because some women just don't know better. God had his hand on me even then. It was called grace. These are some of the very same reasons that when some women get into good relationships they don't know how to handle it and how to treat it because it's not something that they are used to. The only way that we learn is when we welcome God into our lives and He teaches us how to treat our husbands. However, anytime something did happen all I could think about was what did I do wrong, did I lead him on, what could I have done differently. I thought that I had learned the first few times that happened but I guess I didn't because I kept finding myself in the same situation just different people. Just when I thought that I could trust someone they would always do something to make me completely lose the trust that I had. But you know something that I have learned. When you have been trespassed so many times things are stripped from you like your trust in anybody, your security, and not feeling safe is nothing like you have ever felt before. It's like a thief that comes into your house in the middle of the night while you are asleep and take all your belongings and leaves you with nothing. A thief is something else cause he takes so much but yet he leaves you with a lot. He leaves you with no dignity, feeling unsecured, scared all the time, he leaves you with fear. So don't ever say that a thief doesn't leave anything because he does. Molestation and rape or attempted rape can leave you feeling so many ways. Your emotions run wild. I also have felt angry and bitter, mad, wanting to hurt people like they have hurt me. Having thoughts of murder. Just sitting and contemplating and having visions of what that person has done to me and taking their life and why not because it's their fault that I am going through this. I didn't have anyone to talk to at all. I held all this stuff in until I met you. Man stuff like that wears on you especially when you have people who are closed minded and don't understand. People are so judgmental and I don't need and didn't need to feel any worse. People's warped views on things make you feel shameful and feel less than a person, all because they don't understand and have no compassion. Do you know who is the worse ones? "No I don't Kenisha, who", asked David. "Women are. Sometimes we are our own worst enemy. We want to say this about the woman and what she should have or shouldn't have done. It's not all women but you would be shocked about how some women portray that the fault lies with the woman, the victim. Sometimes we get together to put down men because of what certain men has done to us. It's not all men just the messed up ones that we have come encounter with. It makes you wonder what happened to them when they were little kids. Where did they pick up this mentality, how did they grow up, and what did they see. People don't think about all that. All they see is the act, which is understandable. When you dig into their hearts and their lives you will find that what they went through were some similar situations as children that we had been through and never dealt with the situations at hand so a curse is handed down from generation to generation until someone comes along with a made up mind and makes a difference and breaks the curse. Then those are the ones who made right decisions in spite of their circumstances and so God's grace and mercies was upon them. In no ways am I excusing the acts but we have all been victims and it's up to us in which pathway to go. Yes they must take on the responsibility of what they have done but it's also our responsibility to move on as well. Therefore, we as the victims must forgive so that we can move on and stop bringing up the past by continuing to point the finger.

God forgave Paul and he was a murderer of God's people. So who are we to continue to point the finger? It is up to the predator to ask for forgiveness from God and if they don't choose to then they have to live with that. Even if they don't ask us to forgive them we still have to forgive them for ourselves so that we can be free. As long as we stay connected to them by the way of unforgiveness then we will never be free. So, when you think about it, if we had God in our lives from a young age and really had Him as the head of our lives and sought God on dating some these men then we would have saved ourselves from a lot of hurt.

    We as women open ourselves up to hurts and pains when God isn't the head of lives and when His heart has not been sought by us. Proverbs 18:22 says, that *whoso findeth a wife findeth a good thing, and obtaineth favour of the Lord*. We as women need to stay focused in the things of God and our lives and let the men find us instead of the other way around. When we do that we will endure a lot less heartache. David it is just like when we met, I wasn't looking for love but after we got together I don't care what nobody say, it was God, love flourished and I knew after while that you were to be my husband. You knew that I was to be your wife or else you wouldn't have asked me to marry you. In order for us to be free from things of this nature we must be under God's protection. I wish someone had told me that Jesus loved me when I was young. I don't remember anyone ever telling me that Jesus loved me. All I was ever told was to come to church and I felt like why should I go. I can stay out here and do what they are doing. I just wish that someone had told me about Jesus and how He loves me", Kenisha said. "I can't say that I understand because in those issues I don't but I can tell you this, is that you are going to have to make a decision to either wallow in this and continue to live as such for years to come or to go ahead and take the advice that Tyenna and I gave you about talking to our pastors and getting deliverance and guidance", said David. "I know and I will make a decision and I thank you for being truthful with me. Even though you stepped on my toes. I hear you", said Kenisha.

    Kenisha is now at a crossroad. What will she do? God is holding out His hand. Will she smack His hand away or will she embrace what God is trying to do? If you haven't noticed God has been ministering to her all day long. She was pampered. People gave her a baby shower. She got to get some things off her chest and got some encouragement and some guidance. She even got the word occasionally.

    Where are you at right now? Are you at a crossroad? Are you wondering where God is in your life? Well He is here. Right here. What are you going to do about it? Will you receive what He has for you or will you turn Him away? Hebrews 3:15 says, *"while it is said: today, if you will hear His voice, do not harden your hearts as you did in the day of rebellion"*. So hear His voice and take hold of your deliverance, which is what you have been praying for. Did you know that not grabbing God's hand when it is extended to you is in some form rebellion? For example it's like a child, when you hold out your hand and tell the child to come on but the child just stands there and won't come. Doesn't that make you upset? Then you have to go and get the child yourself because you can't leave them there but God is different. If you don't come when He calls then He won't force you. God is a gentleman. He leaves the decision up to you. You can either stay where you are, which is at a standstill and living unhappy. In spite of it all you can make the decision to receive God's word and deliverance, move on and up in God, so that He can take you places that you have never known.

KENISHA'S DELIVERANCE
Chapter 4
"The Word of God"

"Man these boys are heavy", said David. "Why don't you just wake them up and let them walk", Kenisha suggested. "Naw, I am going to let them sleep. I can carry them just unlock and open the door for me so I can get into the house", said David. "Well while you are putting them to bed I will get our clothes ready for church tomorrow", said Kenisha. "Just get the boys clothes and yours. I will choose my own suit", David said. "What! You don't like what I put out for you. Fine then I won't pull out any more clothes for you again", Kenisha said. "Why it gotta be all like that", David said. "You know I'm clownin' you right", Kenisha said. "Yeah I know", David said.

Then they got in the bed and fell right asleep, because of the full day they had. They slept all through the night and were calling the hog's home. David kept messing with her and pinching her nose while she was sleep and he just laughed. Then when he was snoring she pinched his nose and started laughing. The alarm went off at about 6:00 in the morning. Kenisha went about the house waking everybody up. "Get up, get up, and get up", Kenisha yelled! She turned on all the lights and banging on the beds. Then she turned the television on gospel channels and turned it up loud in everybody's room. The boys wouldn't get up so she took them by the legs and pulled them out of bed. They started laughing. Now it's David's turn. "David, get up! David, get your buns out of the bed! David, my water broke, wake up and get me to the hospital! No you didn't just roll over. What if I had been serious and was really in labor", Kenisha said smiling? "I knew you weren't serious cause all you want to do is get me up out of this comfortable bed. I ain't movin", David said. "Fine then, I know how to get you up", said Kenisha. She starts humming down the stairs. Kenisha gets her a big cup of ice-cold water. Then she hums back up the stairs and says, "David are you going to get up"? "Nope, I am not going to get up and if you pour that water on me I am going to get you good", David said. "How did you know that I had a cup of water", Kenisha said laughing? "You forget I know you. I know what you do. Now again, don't pour that water on me or it's on early this morning", as David reassured her. "Well then are you going to get up? That's all I want to know", Kenisha said. "Let me get a few more winks", David said. "You had your few winks when I went downstairs. I am going to give you until the count of 3 then I am going to let it flow. One.., two.., two and a half, three", said Kenisha. Then she began to pour the water over David's head and he grabbed her wrists and they struggled and laughed. He ended up pouring it over her. "Oh my goodness that water is cold", Kenisha screamed! "I told you Kenisha I was going to get you", said David. "That's fine David but I reached my goal because you are up. Watch your back. I will return the favor. I want you to know that", Kenisha said. "Don't worry, I will be watching", said David. They went and got ready for church. "Hey Sweet, you look beautiful this morning", David said. "I already know this. Naw, I'm just kidding, thanks Babe. You are looking mighty fine yourself. I'm goin' to cling tight to you today cause I want the women to know "who you wit", Kenisha said laughing. "Come on Kenisha let's go and get into the car with your silly self. All right, boys let's go", David said. "Hey momma, do we need our coats? No,

Deon. Just get your small jackets. Where are you at Jabreel", Kenisha said? "I'm getting my jacket", Jabreel said. "Do ya'll have your bibles and lessons", said David? "I got mine", Jabreel said. "I can't find mine", said Deon. "It's probably in the truck", David said. "That's why ya'll need to keep your things together in one place so this doesn't happen every time it's time to go to church", David said.

    They all got in the truck and went to church. When they got to church they got out of the car and met and greeted the people of God. "Hey Kenisha, what's up", said Tyenna? "Gurrrl, nothing, but you know I am tired after yesterday. Did you straighten Ricky out", Kenisha said? "Oh you know I handled that. I put him in his place", Tyenna said. They both laughed about it. "God bless Min Langley", Evangelist Franklin said. "God bless you Evangelist Franklin", Minister Langley (Kenisha) said. "Hey Tracy", Kenisha said. "What's crackalackin' Kenisha? You know me just chillin", said Tracy. "I am going to sit right her on the edge of the row cause you know the water be sending back and forth to the restroom", Kenisha said. Deacon Bradshaw said, "Praise the Lord, everybody. We are calling Service to order. How is everyone this morning"? "Blessed", the crowd yelled. "Amen that's what I am talking about. I would like to ask Deaconess Priner to start us off in song", said Deacon Bradsaw? "Hallelujah. Hallelujah. Hallelujah. Hallelujah. Lord we praise you. Lord we praise you. Lord we praise you. Lord we praise you", Deaconess Priner sang. The praise team, offering, and the choir went forth and now they are introducing the pastors of "On Fire For God Ministries". "Introducing to some and presenting to others the pastors of this church Pastors Cleofus and Freida

Rural", announced Sis Dorm.

"Praise the Lord everybody", Pastor Rural said. "Hallelujah", screamed the congregation. "Let me here the congregation praise God in the house today. Let go of yourself and get your mind off your problems and give God the praise. Give God the glory. Give Him the honor. Give Him what He is due. Didn't he bring you out? Didn't He have your back when it was against the wall? Isn't He the one who stuck by you through thick and thin? If He has done anything for you then you should be getting out of your seat and give the cushion a rest", Pastor Rural exalted. The congregation stood and just praised the Lord. There was shouting, dancing, praising, and worshipping going on in the house of the Lord. Then Co-Pastor Rural said, "All right, now let's go before the throne of grace. Lord God we praise you, glorify, and magnify you. We are giving you our hearts and our minds and our very souls today. We are looking for You to confirm some things for us today. Have Your way on today and allow Pastor Rural to decrease as you increase in him to bring forth your word with much clarity, conciseiveness, power, and anointing in the name of Jesus. Lord give him the wisdom on how to bring forth your word. Allow the hearts of your people to receive what thus saith the Lord and whatever hinderance there may be we cast it out of this sanctuary, out of our hearts, and out of our minds in the name of Jesus. Teach us on today Lord and we are forever giving you all the praise and all the honor and all the glory in Jesus name, amen".

Then Pastor Rural came behind Co-Pastor Rural and said, "The title of our lesson on today is, "Learning How To Release My Past". Our scripture basis will be coming from Isaiah 43:18-19 and there will be many other scriptures to follow. Will everyone please turn to Isaiah

43:18-19. I am going to ask my wife to read. Frieda would you please begin"? Co-Pastor Rural begin to read and said, "Yes, sir, Isaiah 43:18-19 (NIV) says, *18, Forget the former things; do not dwell on the past. 19, See, I am doing a new thing! Now it springs up; do you not perceive it?* "Thank you", said Pastor Rural. "Let's ask ourselves why God would want us to forget our past. He says that because He wants us to look forward and be blessed. God said not to dwell in the past. *Dwell means to reside, to inhabit, to rest*. Meaning, that we have made a home for our past to reside in. Have you made a home for your past", asked Pastor Rural? David whispered to Kenisha, "It looks like God is going to be talking to you today huh"? "Whateva David, your toes may get stepped on too", Kenisha said smiling. "Then God says, See, I am doing a new thing! At the end of this sentence He put an exclamation mark, which means excitement. God's excited about the things that He is doing for us and He wants us to be excited too. He then says, now it springs up. In this sentence springs up is an action word, which means it has already started. He is actually doing something. Now God asks, do you not perceive it? He is saying do you not see what I am doing. He wants us to see that He is doing a new thing in us and as long as we keep looking back on the past we will never see what God is doing in our lives and if we are not careful then we will miss it. As long as we keep looking back we will always have a complaint about the state that we are in and it will be harder for us to see a positive future because we keep basing things that is happening to us on what we went through in our past. Now let's talk about what past means, *it is having existed or taken place in a period before the present*. Now, let me stay right here for a minute. Looking at the definition tells us that, yes, something has happened to us and was brought into existence or that we have done something that we knew was wrong. So if it was brought into existence that means that it can become extinct. Extinct means gone, done and over with. The Dictionary says it means, *no longer burning and no longer active, gone out of use, and having no qualified claimant.* Isn't that good news? Let me hear the church say amen", said Pastor Rural! "Amen pastor", yelled the congregation. "Good teaching", said the congregation. "When I was studying this, I was like Jeeeesus! NO QUALIFIED CLAIMANT! Thank you Lord for this enlightenment. I got excited about this thang. Church, do you hear that! It's not qualified to keep us captive any longer. Once we close the doors on our past, that's it. There is no lingering smoke, it doesn't affect us any longer and we are then free. Man, I could end the message on this alone and be done but there are still some things that I need to go more in depth about. Now let's look at the word release. Release means, *to set free from restraint, confinement, or servitude.* My God! Restraint means chains, confinement means prison, and servitude means serving. Are you getting what holding on to your past will do to you? Let's talk about serving for a bit. Serving means, *to answer a need, and to comply with the commands or demands of.* There are many definitions but these were the ones that stuck out to me more. I am here to tell you service that need to hold on to your past no longer! Bring out my illustrators, please. (Picture this). Okay, Bro. Wanks sit at the table. He is the customer and Bro. Thomb is the waiter. Now Bro Wanks snap your fingers and call the waiter. He snaps his fingers and says, "excuse me waiter but I have been sitting here for 30 minutes and no one has taken my order". Then, Bro Thomb came to the customer and said, "sir, I am sorry for the wait.

What would you like to order"? Now, do ya'll see what just happened? The waiter had to comply with the commands and or the demands of the customer. He became subject to the customer. He had to answer the need, as so stated in the dictionary. This is the same thing that holding on to our past will do to us. Every time we try and move forward, here come our past, snapping it's fingers, calling us, commanding us to come subject to it. If we continue to let our past be our dictator then it will have us doing things that we thought that we would never do. We hear people all the time say to us, I remember when you use to do this, but our reply has to be, yes, I did use to do that but I don't do those things anymore. I work for God now and my affections are set on things above. We can't allow anyone to keep us thinking about the things that we used to do. We also can't allow the enemy to keep us thinking about what someone has done to us", said Pastor Rural. "Say that, shouted", Sis Barlow. "Amen", some of the congregation shouted. "Keeping things about previous times in our hearts is dangerous. We bring so many different spirits along with us and some are so slick they stay hidden, so subtle, and sneaks up on us and we don't realize it until we do something that we never thought we would do. If you asked some prisoners how did they get there and most will probably say, "I don't know", because they committed a crime that they never thought that they would do. I am not making excuses for them but if you looked in their past you could probably see where it stemmed from.

Let's use anger. The bible says *be angry and sin not. Do not let the sun go down while you are still angry. (Eph 4:26 NIV)* God says that because if you go to sleep angry, you will wake up angry. Can you imagine being sleep and letting the spirit of anger manifest for at least 8 hours", asked Pastor Rural? "My God, yelled", Min Spokes. "That's a long time to let something manifest", said Pastor Rural. "Yes it is", yelled Sis Minnks. "Think of it this way. Eight hours is a workday and in that workday you accomplish a workload. Now think about the enemy is at work too and the best time for him to work is while we are yet sleep.

You see when we are not following God's word; we have given the enemy something to work with and a lot more can be created. So be obedient. What we have to realize is that we won't know anything until all of a sudden we notice that we went from being angry to being bitter. Being angry is not a sin but when it becomes sin is when we act on it in the negative. Here is something that may help you a little better to understand. Anger is past tense, which means that we have allowed it to linger and haven't let it go. Angry is present tense, which means that it hasn't taken root so we can take care of the situation at its' lowest level. I hope we all got that", said Pastor Rural. "Amen pastor", yelled some of the congregation. "Preach pastor", Kenisha yelled. Tyenna looked back shaking her head and said with a smile on her face, "You ought to be shamed. Stop playing because you know God is talking to you". "I know right", Kenisha said. "I want you to look at Joseph. In Genesis 45:3-5 (MSG) read it on your own time. I am going to just skim over it for the sake of time. *Joseph reveals who he is to his brothers and he told them not to feel badly and not to blame themselves for selling him. He then said God was behind it. God sent me here ahead of you to save lives.* Joseph is the very epidimy of what forgiving really is. Now, I know that he had to be angry about what happened to him. Being sold into slavery is no punk. That's some serious stuff. He saw the bigger picture though. He saw God in it and realized God's plan for his life and what he was to do. We all need to see that. We all need to see that God is at work in our lives. Life can bring some punches but God's word teaches us to be strong so that we can take some punches and be able to counter attack the punches thrown. We have to know who we are in Christ. Once we know and believe that then we can conquer everything. I want to tell you a story about a little boy. This all has to do with us releasing our past. Just like Joseph, life hands us some things and we have to know how to release it and love at a greater level. Like I said, I am going to tell you a story about a little boy and what happened to him and how he overcame it all.

There was a little boy and at the age of seven he was molested, says Pastor Rural. Tyenna looks back at Kenisha and says, "is he all up in our conversation or what"? Kenisha said, "you know". Then Pastor Rural continues with his message and says, "Now the act has been committed. Confusion has hit this little boy because it was a man that did it to him. He is now quiet when he used to be joyful and a rambunctious character. He doesn't tell a soul. The child is scared and no one notices the sudden change in him. Once he felt secure and now he no longer does. Where was his safety? This act happened at his home. At one time he could tell his parents about anything but now he is ashamed. Who could he trust? Another man? Of course not. Sex has been taught to a child who once knew nothing about it. A child who once felt good about himself now feels lower than dirt and this is as time moves on. Years begin to past and this thing is still being done to him. He shuts himself off to the world. No one understands his pain. Now the person is gone and he still tells no one. His mom doesn't understand why he is so angry. "Why is my son so bitter when I didn't raise him that way", his mom thought? He puts on a mask so that no one will know who he really is. (By this time Kenisha's eyes is filled with tears.) He goes through years of this and begins to question is sexuality. All this boy knows is that he has had sex with this man for years unwillingly, so why change now. Because his mother was a church going momma his eyes were opened that marriage is for man and woman only because he has read Genesis 2:20-25. But, there was also something that would never let him go that way. He didn't know it at the time but it was God. He didn't understand what that was but he knew that a gay relationship was not of God (according to many scriptures, for example, Romans 1:24-27). Let's be real, when dealing with same sex relationships it has stemmed from somewhere. No one wakes up saying that this is how I want to be. It can stem from so many things for example, molestation or broken home. A boy child that really needed a male figure in his life but didn't have one. So he grew up around women and he clinged only to what he knew, or people spoke it on you because of how your character was when you was a child. So for you parents, stop speaking curses upon your children and stop allowing other people to speak mess and curses upon your children because of something that a child might do. Parents we have a responsibility to our children to protect them from all things especially spoken curses over their lives. If we lift our children up in the home meaning not beating them down with words as to where their spirits are broken, then no one will be able to infiltrate what you have already instilled into them. It starts in the home.

Another thing too, STOP CALLING THEM BAD!!!! If you notice that is a curse! It burns me up on the inside when I hear people say that a child is bad. Children are not bad they have just made some wrong choices but it is not who they are. Our children are just in training. I am sorry for getting off into this but this must be said. I will get back to the story. Think of a soldier when they enter into basic training. They don't know what they are doing. They have to be taught. And when they are taught and keep making mistakes or wrong choices there is corrective training, but that doesn't make them bad soldiers. Also look at it like this, who are their trainers. What are their trainers doing? Are they training in accordance to regulations or are they training their own way and forgot about instructions? Sometimes you have to look at the trainers or drill sergeants and the same with parenting. When our children do something wrong look back at yourself and see have you been disobedient to God in any way. When we are not training our children, we are giving up on them. We give them up to so many things, spirits, and people. Proverbs 22:6 say, *Train up a child in the way he should go; and when he is old he will not depart from it.* So yes, for all you naysayers, they are in training. Think about it like this, God's people; think about what you used to do in the past, does that make you a bad person just because of a wrong choice that you made. So now let me let you ponder on this, why isn't it the same justification for our babies. Our babies aren't bad. It's our jobs as parents to correct them when they make a mistake. We love our children into the kingdom of God. We love them into our arms. I don't know why God took me that way church but obviously someone had to hear that. So let's make this u-turn back to the subject at hand. I knew I wasn't going to get too many amen's behind that but it's okay. That just lets me know that spirit is in the house and it needed to be dealt with", said Pastor Rural. Some of the congregation smiled while gritting their teeth and some others just laughed. "You say that pastor", said Co-pastor Rural. "Thank you Baby. I always know that you got my back. All right, so in any event, back to the story. Here is now a man in physical form due to time, but the child is still inside locked up and balled up because he hasn't been released to grow up mentally. The child in him that is hurt so badly because of years of abuse now wants to be released. This man wants to be free. I know about this cause this was once me. Can we be obedient to the Holy Spirit church", asked Pastor Rural? "Amen pastor", the congregation responded.

Chapter 5
"The Altar Call"

"God has dropped in my spirit that there is a woman here who is experiencing exactly what I am talking about. There may be some differences in there somewhere but for the most part there is truth to it. Come up here for prayer. Be obedient to the Spirit of the Living God.

Now at this time Kenisha has tears flowing down her face while her husband David is holding her and Tyenna looks back at her and says, "Kenisha you need to go and be obedient". David said, "Baby you know that God is speaking to you. You have to go by faith. If He has given the pastor all of this, you know that it is God". Kenisha listened and continued to sit there as Pastor Rural offered the invitation. Her mind was going 100 miles an hour. She knew that God was tugging at her heart and yet she sat there because the devil was telling her that people would look at her different if she went, and that her life would be an open book. All she could think about is what would people say if they knew that I had these issues.

Pastor Rural said, "Come on now. Don't let the devil keep you from making a decision to give it to God so that you can go forth in your deliverance. Make your decision today. God is stretching out to you. Don't reject Him. He has also given me your name so I know who you are but you are going to have to do this thing by faith. He also told me that the devil has you thinking that people will look at you differently. Well wonder no longer cause everyone in here has a past other wise we wouldn't be here. Please come on up, he said as he looked straight into her eyes and held out his hand. David said, "Kenisha go". Kenisha stood up and walked very slowly. That was the longest walk she has ever taken. It was like walking the green mile. Fear tried to grip her but FAITH kept her moving. Pastor Rural said, "Give her a handclap of praise. Her faith is going to make her whole. By this time, her eyes were puffy and tears were falling like raindrops. She was crying uncontrollably. She got to altar, stretched her arms wide, looked up and cried out to Jesus. Co-Pastor came and stood by her because God had allowed them to see and feel her pain. Then Pastor Rural said, "there is deliverance at the altar. I know that we didn't get through the whole lesson but let's let God have his way. If you want God to be the head of your life, please come. If you have anything from your past that torments you, keeps you up at night, or keeps you from moving forward in the things of God. Please come. There is a Holy Ghost arrest in this place. Let God deliver you. God has said that, "He wants to do a new thing and that you are to forget the former things". Which means, God has something for you to do and it is time for you to come forth, in the name of Jesus. It's your time. It's your season. He wants to take some old things from you and put some new things in you and I think about the scripture, St. Matthew 9:17-16 that says, *No man putteth a piece of new cloth unto an old garment, for that which is put in to fill it up taketh from the garment, and the rent is made worse. Neither do men put new wine into old bottles: else the bottles break, and the wine runneth out, and the bottles perish: but they put new wine into new bottles, and both are preserved.* God is saying in those scriptures that, in order for Him to do this new thing, you must first be made whole. In other words get delivered. As Pastor Rural is speaking, people are walking down the isle crying and sobbing, making their way to the altar. The song stress is singing mildly in the background, "Where are you in

Christ, where are you in Christ, you ought to know, where are you in Christ. Pastor continued to minister saying, "yes God wants you delivered so that He can do a new thing in you and when He does it you will be preserved and nothing will leak out but you must get delivered first so that He can set you free. Come and give it to Him. Once you release it to Him then the healing and the process can begin but first you must give Him your cares, ALL OF THEM! The ministers are coming. My leaders, if you have not been on your face praying then don't come up here praying over people. This is a serious thing and God needs people who have truly been on their face and being intimate with Him. There are needs on this altar and so we can't play games up here. Those that are on the altar raise your hand and repeat after me. Lord, "Lord", Please help me "please help me", I need you "I need you" to come into my areas that were once closed off to you (and they continued to repeat after him). Cleanse me Lord. I want you to invade my space and make me whole. I desire change. I want change. *I know that in all these things I am more than a conqueror through Him (Christ Jesus) that loved us (Romans 8:37)*. Ministers begin to pray with the people on the altar and come into agreement with them. Pastor Rural came to Kenisha and specifically prayed for her. He begin to pray for her and said, Lord you see the needs of your woman servant. We ask for healing for her soul, healed of hurts and past pains, healed in the mental capacity. Healing in every area of her life. Help her to release her past in the mighty name of Jesus. Help her to release the people that have done her harm. Show her how to forgive them and herself. There is no more low self-esteem. There is no more insecurities, no more fear in the name of Jesus. Fear has to let go. Your word, God, says that if she submits to you and resist the devil then he will flee from her. She has submitted to You by coming to the altar and asking for Your help. Build up boldness and humility in her right now in the name of Jesus. Let the fruit of the spirit manifest in her life. Give her sight that she may see an instant change in her life. Take the scales off her eyes in the mighty name of Jesus. Open Your word up to her and increase her prayer life with You in the name of Jesus. Touch her like never before. When Pastor Rural said that, Kenisha fell back on the floor, slained in the spirit. God had His way. She got up off the floor after a few minutes and cried out to God. Thank You! Thank You! God I love You! Lord I praise you! Jesus, I thank You! Jesus there is none like You! She continued to cry out and shouted and danced before the Lord. "God's presence is surely in this place. Deliverance is surely in this place", said Pastor Rural. Other people at the altar was crying out and shouting too. The Spirit of the Living God just saturated the church. People in their seats begin to leap and people crying out to God from one end of the church to the other. The musicians had to come off their instruments. They couldn't even hold it any longer. God did a new thing in the church that day. People were healed, set free, and delivered. Some repented. God had done something in them that they have never experienced before. They didn't know that it could be like this. It was truly a move of God. After everything had calmed down Pastor Rural said, "God showed up and showed today, didn't He"! The congregation yelled, "hallelujah"! "Please don't let this be a high but go home and let God minister to you even more. He has so much more that He wants to say to you. We are going to go ahead and close out service because the time has been well spent. I don't even want announcements done. Check your emails tomorrow morning for all the announcements. I want God's presence to continue in the spirit that it is now. We can't even stop the tears from falling from our eyes. I want the musicians to play a worshipping song until people have cleared out of the sanctuary. So that means get your stuff and head out while the Lord is still ministering. Be obedient, amen". The congregation said, "amen". "God bless you all", said Pastor Rural.

    The service ended and people grabbed their things and their children. It was just quiet as they left the sanctuary. Some got into their cars and left still crying and some stayed out in the parking lot talking about the service and laughing and enjoying God and each other. Kenisha just went to her Denali and sat and just continued to be ministered to by God. David gathered the children and grabbed the bags and came on to the Denali. He said, "Kenisha are you good"? "Yes David I am good. I just wanted to have some time to myself so that God can finish ministering to me that's all", she said. "Do you need more time", David said? "No, I am fine now, besides if you go back in the church I wouldn't be able to get you out", she said smiling. "Hey Kenisha, Pastor and Co-Pastor Rural want to see you and David", Tyenna said. "Can you keep an eye on the boys for us", David asked? "Yeah but if it's going to be a while, I will just take them home with us and ya'll can pick them up on your way home", answered Tyenna. "Okay that's straight. So if I don't see the Montero then I know that ya'll have left. I will call your cell phone. I hope that it doesn't take long cause a sista is hungra", Kenisha said jokingly. "Girl you are something else", Tyenna said. "I try to be", said Kenisha. "Come on Kenisha we can't stand here and continue to talk to short people in the parking lot. You know cars can't see her", David said.

"Whateva David cause if it was nighttime cars couldn't see you either", Tyenna said. "Ya'll are off tha chain", Kenisha said. "Come on David let's go see what the pastors want. We will get up with you in a minute Tyenna", Kenisha said. "I will get you back later Tyenna", said David. "I will wait on it", said Tyenna.

They walked to the pastors' office and knocked on the door. Then the armor bearers let them in. "You wanted to see us sir", David said. "Yes, come in and have a seat. This won't take long. I just wanted Kenisha to know that if ever you need to talk to get through these things please don't hesitate to get with the administrator and schedule an appointment to see us. I know how the enemy works. He makes you think that no one will understand how you feel and too shameful to talk about it but we are here for you", said Pastor Rural. "Thank you Pastor and Co-Pastor Rural. I appreciate that", said Kenisha. "One thing that we want you to know is that before you come to us we want you to go to God first because we are going to ask you if you did when you come in the office. Keep God first and He will lead and direct you. We are not to be your crutch but we do want to be a help. God will lead you when to schedule an appointment with us. You know how we do things here. We are not going to baby you but we will help you. God has shown us the ministry in the both of you so you really and truly have to lean solely on God. We are your pastors and we want you to feel comfortable in knowing that, we are here to guide you, all right", Pastor Rural said. "Yes sir, we understand", David said. "Kenisha you are going to have to stay in prayer and let God minister to you. Take the time this week and really seek the face of God. He wants to show you a lot of things but you have to be in position for Him to show you and take you there. You received your deliverance today but if you don't stay in prayer you won't keep it. Maintain your deliverance and you already know how to do that", said Co-Pastor Rural. "Yes ma'am I do", Kenisha responded. "I know that you already know that you will be tested to see if you have stuck by your decision, so remember to take hold of God anytime you see or feel that your decision is being tested", said Pastor Rural. "All right. I got you sir. I am going to stand firm on my decision to be free and to keep my past released from me", Kenisha said. "Amen. Well that's all I wanted to say to you guys. Ya'll have a blessed day and get full cause I am getting ready to", said Pastor Rural laughing. "Thank you sir", said Kenisha. They all laughed and gave each other a hug and went about their day. Tyenna and the boys were still out in the parking lot talking. So they grabbed them and said bye to everyone. Now David and Kenisha are in the car talking. "So where do you want to go eat", David asked? "I hadn't really thought about it. What did you have a taste for", Kenisha asked? "I am in the mood for some Chinese food", David said. "That's cool. I can live with that", said Kenisha. "Let's go to the one by the grocery store. They usually have fresh food on the buffet", said Kenisha. "Alright", David said. "Hey boys we are going to eat Chinese food for dinner", said David. "Yahhh"! the kids screamed. "David it looks like it is packed over here", she said. "I know but we will be alright cause I ain't goin' anywhere else. A brotha is hungry", he said. "Mannnn, I feel you. Let me out while you park so I can get us a table before these people get out of their cars", she said. "I will see you on the inside", said David. "Hello, welcome to King of China. How many is with your party?" the waitress said. "Four altogether and non-smoking please", said Kenisha. "Follow me, please", said the waitress. The waitress placed her and then David and the boys came in. David what do you want to drink? I am going to get ice tea. "I think I am too," Kenisha said. "I am going to get the boys sprite", David said. Then another waitress came after a few minutes and said, "Hello, my name Sue and I will be your waitress this afternoon". Here are your drinks and you can go ahead to the buffet". "Okay, thank you", David said. They went on and finished their meals and left and they got home and took a nap.

Chapter 6
"Delivering The Baby"

"Jesus!" Kenisha screamed. "What's wrong", David asked. "A contraction just hit and boy did that one hurt", she said. "Is that the first one Kenisha", David asked? "I was sleep and all that I know is that this one woke me up out of my sleep. "Okay Kenisha, here we go. It's time to actually time these contractions to see what we are dealing with", said David. "What do you mean to see what we are dealing with", she asked? "What I mean is, are you having contractions or braxton hicks", he answered. "Watch some television girl while we time these contractions", he said. "Ain't nothin' on. Can you put a movie in the DVD player", she asked? "I gotcha. I am going to put in something funny, okay", he said. "You are really trying to send me into labor with something funny huh, she said. "Jesus", Kenisha yelled! "You just had another one huh", he asked? "Uh huh", she said. "We are going to time it for at least 30 minutes okay", he said. "That's fine David. While we are waiting the boys can pack their clothes and things so they can get ready to go over Rick and Tyenna's house. Can you call them and give them a heads up", she said? "I got you Kenisha", he said. David called for the boys, "Jabreel and Deon come here"! "Yes sir", the boys responded. "Hey boys we believe the baby is coming so ya'll go and pack your clothes, brushes and combs, toothbrushes, and anything else that you need", he told them. "Okay daddy", they answered. "Mommy are you okay," Deon asked? "Yes baby I am fine. Make sure that ya'll use your duffle bags. "All right mommy," the children said. "Yes Lord Jesus," Kenisha said. "It's another one", he asked? "Yes David", she said. "Okay sweetheart just breath. Let me call Rick", he said. "Here's the phone David", Kenisha said. After he dialed the phone number, he said, "Hey Rick this is David". "What's goin' on man", Rick said. "Well we are going to be heading to the hospital in the next half hour. Kenisha is having contractions and they are consistent. I was calling to let you know that the arrangement that we made about the boys is now ready to be activated", said David. "Man, you know that's straight. You did not have to go through all that. Just say that they are coming because you all are headed to the hospital", said Rick. "You know me. I am going to be as clear and concise as I can be", David said. "Yeah well ya'll just be on your way and I will let Tyenna know", Rick said. "All right, we will see you guys then", said David. "Bye", said Rick. "Kenisha is there anything that you need or want before we head to the hospital", David asked. "Yeah, I am going to take a shower and I need to go over my bag one more time to see if I have everything. Could you get me some ice cubes cause I won't be able to eat anything", she said? "Yeah, I'll make sure you have everything in your bag and I will get you some ice cubes in a cup. Let me go check on the boys and see what they are doing. I am going to have to check their bags as well because I know they forgot something. You go and take your shower and I will have some sweats laid out here for you. Deon let me check your bag. Where are your pajamas", David asked? "I didn't put any in the bag", Deon said. "Put you some in here. Other than that it looks like you have everything else. Jabreel let me see what's in your bag. You need some pajamas too and your belt. Do ya'll want to take some games with you", their dad asked? "Yes", they answered. "Pack what games you want to take but remember to bring back everything you take. Do ya'll understand", he said? "Yes daddy", the children said. "Get your shoes on and get ready to go. We are going to be taking your mom to the hospital to have the baby. We are going to drop ya'll off at Rick's house so ya'll can play with Nick. Let me go and check on your momma. Hey Kenisha are you okay", he asked? "Yes David, I am fine", she said. "Have you had any more contractions", he asked? "Yeah and they are getting worse", she said. "Just take it easy. I got the boys straight and now I am getting ready to check your bag and get you some ice cubes and we will be heading out", he said. David checked the bags and got her some ice cubes and they left. They drove over Rick and Tyenna's house and dropped off Jabreel and Deon and while David was inside making sure that they were okay Kenisha's water broke. She called him on his cell phone and said, "Baby my water just broke". "He said I am on my way out. All right ya'll her water broke. I got to go", said David. "Yeah man hurry up and take her cause you know she so short that she will drown in the truck just by her water breaking. Ya'll make sure that you call us and let us know what is going on", Rick said. "Man you know you ain't right talkin' about my baby like that. I am going to tell her too. She needs to hear something that will make her smile. Bye ya'll", David said. "Bye", said Rick and Tyenna. "Come on baby let's ride and get you to the hospital. Just remember to breath baby", David said. "I know to breath. Just drive and get me to the hospital", she said. "Kenisha you are going to owe me big once this baby comes. You will serve me breakfast in bed for how you are treating me. By the way when you called me on your cell phone to tell me that your water broke, Rick cracked a joke and said, that I better hurry up and because you are so short that you will drown in the car just by your water breaking", he said. "David let me tell you somethin' right now I am in a lot of pain so I am going to let that one slide and Rick knows that he has it coming. Just park over here so we can get out", she said. When they got there David and Kenisha got settled in their room. The doctors gave Kenisha an I.V. and drew blood and hooked her up to all types of machines. It came time for her to push. "David will you hold my hand", she said? "Here baby don't worry. I am here", he said. "Okay Mrs. Langley, on the count of 3 I want you to push. One, two, three push", the doctor said. Kenisha pushed and she pushed and she pushed some more. Then finally the doctor gave up and said, "Mr. and Mrs. Langley we are going to have to do an emergency c-section". "Why", asked David? "Well Mr. Langley her pelvic area is too small and every time she pushes the baby comes down but when she stops pushing he goes back up and it is causing distress on the baby", the doctor told him. After Kenisha went through the c-section the doctor said, "Mr. and Mrs. Langley congratulations on your new baby girl"!

KENISHA'S FREEDOM
Chapter 7
"Stepping Into Purpose"

Kenisha is in the hospital recovering from her c-section. David is by her side and made all the necessary phone calls to the baby girl's grandparents and friends. They named the baby Cheyenne Faith Langley. She is 5lbs.6oz. and 21 inches long. She is so tiny and a beautiful baby. She has a head full of black curly hair. She has black eyes with long eyelashes. Her skin is a light brown color. The nurse came in and did Kenisha's vitals and said, "The doctor will be in momentarily". Then she left. So after a few minutes the doctor came in and said, "While your daughter was in the nursery they noticed her breathing wasn't normal. So they have put her in NICU. Don't be alarmed. We just want to take the necessary precautions to make sure that she is all right. She is in an incubator. She is being fed in through a tube. Also, for right now you won't be able to hold her. Now you guys can go see her but no matter what you see just know that we are only taking precautions and that she is okay. If you have any questions concerning her care, then please don't hesitate to ask". "Where is the NICU wing", asked David? "When you come out of your room, turn left. Then go down by the double doors and make a right. It will be the first room on your left. Just show them your admittance wristband and they will take you to your daughter", the doctor said. "Thank you sir," said Kenisha. "Now Mrs. Langley you will have to go down and walk with your I.V. so the nurse will be in to unhook it so that you can walk with your I.V. I will send her in as soon as I leave", the doctor stated. "Okay sir", Kenisha said. "Hey

Kenisha let me get your robe so that you can put it on. While we are waiting for the nurse to come in, we could be getting ready", David said. "That's fine David. I see you are just as eager to see Cheyenne as I am", Kenisha said. "Of course I am", David responded. "Okay Mrs. Langley, I am going to wrap this cord around this pole and you should be able to walk with it with no problem", the nurse said. "Thank you ma'am", Kenisha said. "David are you ready to go", Kenisha asked? "Yes, but I want you to take it easy. Please walk carefully Kenisha", he said with concern. "I am David. Trust me I am going to be very careful. I am not going to hurt myself. I am in enough pain as it is. I tell you what though; I thank God for the perceset. That is some good medicine", she said. "Girl you are something else. Come on and let's go", he said. They both laughed and began to walk down to see their daughter. They showed the nurses the wristband and they led them down to where Cheyenne was.

    When they got there they couldn't believe their eyes. Kenisha's eyes immediately filled up with tears. She heard what the doctor said but what she seen was something totally different. All she could see was that there was tubes everywhere. There were tubes in her forehead, foot, and in her nose. All they could do was hold her hand through the holes in the incubator. Kenisha gripped David and he was quiet. David didn't say much. He just held Cheyenne's hand with one hand and held onto Kenisha with the other. David squeezed Kenisha's hand. She only seen David cry one other time since they had been together and that was when his grandfather died and now she sees a tear drop from his eye. Will I ever know how he felt that day is what she thought? Then all of a sudden she thought about what she kept saying throughout her pregnancy, "I don't want a girl". She told David, "Stay here with Cheyenne and I will be right back". "Where are you going Kenisha", David asked? "I have to go to the room to do something. I will be right back", she said. "Will you be all right walking back to the room by yourself," he enquired? "Yeah. This is my 3rd time so I am used to it now", she said. "Okay don't be long other wise I will be coming to look for you", he said. "I will be back", she said. Kenisha walked to the room. She laid on her bed and began to cry out, "My God! Please forgive me for saying that I didn't want a little girl. I was just afraid. I didn't really mean it. Please forgive me Lord Jesus. I didn't realize until know that what I speak is so powerful. I want my little girl. I love her. I just didn't want her to go through what I went through. I have been through a lot and I just don't want that for her. Lord, teach me how to raise my child in the admonition of You Lord. Jesus I ask that you intervene on the behalf of Cheyenne in the name of Jesus. *By His stripes* Cheyenne is healed in the name of Jesus! Lord I cry out to you. Please hear my cry. I will walk in the path that You have set for me. This is a vow between You and I. Just save her life. Regulate her breathing in the name of Jesus! God I know that you are all powerful and I believe that you can do this thing. I bind the hand of the enemy in this situation right now in the name of Jesus. Lord God send in the Holy Ghost in the name of Jesus! I know that my baby has angels assigned to her and I dispatch them right now in the name of Jesus! She can't pray for herself but I can pray for her on her behalf. You said in Jeremiah 30:17 that *you will restore unto* Cheyenne *health and heal her wounds and this you declared*. I dispatch the healing angels to restore my baby in the name of Jesus. I know that we are to come to you to be healed of our sicknesses. Therefore, I declare this day and this hour that Cheyenne is healed in the name of Jesus! I command the enemy to go in the name of Jesus! I have been snared by the words of my mouth but the love for my child will cover the multitude of sinful thoughts in the name of Jesus! I have prayed this prayer in faith. In Jesus name, amen. She wiped her eyes and went back to David and Cheyenne. "I was on my way to come and find you. Kenisha what was you doing", David said? "I went back to the room to pray and ask for forgiveness of my sins and thoughts towards having a little girl. If I had never thought it or spoke it Cheyenne wouldn't be in this mess now", she said. At least you repented and got it right with God. I need to ask for forgiveness for never correcting you when you would say it. Here I will let you spend some time with her while I go and do some praying myself. I will be back", he said. "That's straight David. I will see you when you get back", she said. David left and went to the room and prayed as well. Kenisha just looked at her baby and seen what her words did to their little girl. But she got her thoughts together and said, "I repented and God forgave me and it's time for me to forgive myself. My daughter is healed in Jesus name and by the blood of the Lamb", said Kenisha while praying quietly. Other mother's seen her praying over Cheyenne. They just watched her. A nurse looked out the door and watched her as well. They could see a look of calmness over Kenisha. The Lord spoke to Kenisha and said, "I am using this situation right now and I am going to turn it around for your good. Remember this moment. Watch your surroundings." "Yes Lord," Kenisha said. After a while David came back and Kenisha said, "man you talk about me but you little long winded yourself". "You are something else but the Lord did tell me something", David said. "What did He tell you", Kenisha asked? "He told me that He was going turn the situation around for our good", David said. "Oh my gosh, He said the same thing to me while you were praying", she said. "I don't know what He is going to do Kenisha but I can't wait. I am excited about the whole thing", he said. "I am excited too David". "Are you okay Sweet", he asked? "Yeah I am okay. I think that I have been standing up for too long and the pain medication is wearing off", she said. "I will walk you back to the room. Then I will come back down here and sit with Cheyenne while you rest", he said. "That will be cool because I am getting a little tired as well", she said. Kenisha kissed her finger and touched Cheyenne and said, " I will be back after I get some rest. I love you." David walked her back to the room and called the nurse for some more pain medication. Kenisha soon fell off to sleep and David went back down to spend time with Cheyenne. As Kenisha was sleep God gave her a dream. Kenisha was in a Malt-Wartz parking lot. She was getting a cart from the cart bin in the parking lot for her daughter. As she walked back to the truck an angel of the Lord appeared unto her. She couldn't see the face. The angel's face was covered. He said, "I am an angel of the Lord and the Lord has sent me to ask you something and this is your last chance to accept this calling and if you don't accept then evil things will befall you. You have to promise that you will teach and take care of the girls. Do you promise?" Kenisha said, "yes I promise". Then she woke up. "Awwh man, that was a wild dream. I wonder what it means. I need to write this down so that I can remember it and pray for the interpretation", Kenisha said. She wrote it down and prayed. "Lord I am not sure what this dream means and what it entails. I am not sure and have no clarity. The one thing that I am sure is that I am supposed to be doing a work for You but what is it exactly. I don't want anything evil to befall me. I want to walk in Your way and do Your will in the name of Jesus. There is nothing that I want more than to do what You have purposed for me to do. I don't want to miss a step in the name of Jesus. Put me on the path that You have chosen for my life. Order my steps in the name of Jesus. Lead me in every direction to bring me to the ultimate path in the name of Jesus. Give me the interpretation of this dream in Jesus name I pray. Amen", Kenisha prayed. Then the phone rang. "Hello", Kenisha answered. "Hey girl what's up", said Tyenna? "Nothing much but sitting here resting. How are the boys and they better not be giving you and Rick any trouble", Kenisha said. "Girl they are fine and you know that. They don't give us trouble and if they do then you know that we will handle that. How is Cheyenne", Tyenna asked? "She is in NICU", Kenisha answered. "Why? What happened", Tyenna asked with concern? "Well the doctor said that her breathing was irregular and they wanted to see what was going on with her", Kenisha said. "Well Kenisha we know that she is healed in Jesus name", Tyenna said. "Yeah girl. Already prayed tha prayer and so did David. It was hard for us at first because all we seen were tubes going through our baby's forehead and other tubes going into other parts of her body. Then we can't hold her right now because she is in an incubator and we can only touch her through the holes on the incubator. Cheyenne is being fed through a feeding tube right now", Kenisha said. "All is well. We know what we believe, right Kenisha", Tyenna said. "Yeah girl I gotcha. Like I said we have already prayed the prayer of faith and there is no going back", Kenisha said. "I was going to ask you if ya'll wanted us to bring the boys up there to see their baby sister but I ain't so sure now", said Tyenna. "Naw, I don't want them to see her like that. They can see her when she comes home", Kenisha said. "That's cool Kenisha. I can understand that. Do you mind if Rick and I come up there while Arie watches the boys", she said? "Yeah, ya'll can come and see Cheyenne", Kenisha said. "Well we will be up there in about an hour", Tyenna said. "All right Tyenna we will see ya'll then, bye", she said. "Bye, Kenisha", Tyenna said. "I see that you are up", David said. "Yeap, I'm up. How is Cheyenne doing", she asked? "She is sleep right now. She looks so cute sleeping. I can't wait until they take those tubes out of her though', he said. "I know what you mean David", she said. "You know while I was sleep I had this dream", she said. "What was it about", he said? "I was in Malt-Wartz parking lot and I was getting out of the truck. I went to the back of the truck and an angel of the Lord appeared unto me. I couldn't see the face of the angel. Then he said, "I am an angel of the Lord and the Lord has sent me here to ask you something and this is your last chance to accept this calling and if you don't then evil things will befall you. You have to promise that you will teach and take care of the girls. Do you promise? Then I said, "yes I promise". After that I woke up. What do you think it means", she asked him? "I don't know sweetheart. Kenisha just keep praying and asking God to reveal to you the interpretation. Was that Tyenna on the phone", David said? "Yeah it was. They are on their way up here in about another hour", she said. "Are they bringing the boys", he asked? "No, I told her not to because I didn't want them to see their baby sister the way that she is", she said. "That's good Kenisha cause I was thinking the same thing", he said. "Do you want to go home and get some rest baby", Kenisha asked? "Yeah, I think I better. I can go and change clothes and get a few hours of sleep then I will be back up here", David said.

"Okay baby. You go home and get you some good sleep. Kisses", she said. "I love you Kenisha", he said. "I love you too David", he said. "I will be back later", he said. Kenisha changed pajamas and put on her robe and waited for Rick and Tyenna to come up so she could take them down to see Cheyenne. She just watched television and answered the million phone calls she received from family and friends. Her parents said that they were coming down for a week to visit. Kenisha really looked forward to seeing them. She loves it when her parents come down to visit. The nurse came in to do her vital signs and to check on her incision. As the nurse was leaving Rick and Tyenna walked in. "Heeeeyyy new mommy"! yelled Tyenna. "Wuz up girl! How you doin' Rick", Kenisha said? "You know me, just layin' back and chillin' in tha cut", Rick said. "Man can't you just say you doin' good? Dog Tyenna you need to check that. Teach him how to answer a question", Kenisha said jokingly. "I know right", Tyenna said. "See I need David here to put you in yo' place cause when he ain't around you don't be knowin' how to act", Rick said. "Uh uh get him Tyenna. If I could get off this bed and get a hold of him myself I would but I can't so handle that for me would you please", said Kenisha. "Girl you know I got you", said Tyenna. "Are ya'll ready to see Cheyenne", Kenisha asked? "Well I know you know we did not come to see you", said Rick. "Uh uh see how about you stay here while I take Tyenna. Naw I am just playin'. Come on ya'll let's go. I have to walk a little slow so bear with me", Kenisha said. "Believe me it won't be a change cause as short as your legs are we are use to you walkin' slow", Rick said teasingly." I know you ain't goin' there. Your wife is the same height as me so don't play", Kenisha said. "See I wasn't even in tha mix. How you gone bring me into it", Tyenna said? "Sorry Ty, he was tryin' to play me. You ought to be offended yourself cause he tried to clown you without sayin' it. Think about it you are the same height as me and then he said that he was used to it. Girl think about it", she said. "Kenisha you ain't right but you do have a point", she said. "Don't trip Tyenna cause you gotta go home with me", Rick said. "Shoot Kenisha you always gettin' somebody in trouble", Tyenna said sounding like a five year old. "Well ya'll here she is. Like I said we couldn't hold her but we can hold her hands through the holes in the incubator", Kenisha said. "Look at her Rick. She is so cute", Tyenna said. "Yeah I see", said Rick. "I know she looks like me doesn't she", Kenisha said? "NO SHE DOESN'T"! Rick said jokingly. "Why you got to say it like that"? Kenisha said laughingly. "Naw Kenisha, I am sorry girl but right about now she is looking like her daddy", she said. "Tyenna we ain't goin' to be friends if you keep making comments like that", Kenisha said. "Well what do you want me to do, lie to you? I am a Christian and I cannot tell a lie", Tyenna said.

They all continued to laugh and joke around and what was more important they were not focused on what was going on in the natural because spiritually it was already done. Rick and Tyenna didn't even comment on all the tubes that were on Cheyenne and that made Kenisha feel so good. Tyenna and Rick left and Kenisha stayed with Cheyenne for a while just holding her hand, smiling and talking to her. She read bible stories to her and watched her. She couldn't wait for the time to arrive that she could hold her baby. That's all she kept speaking. Kenisha kept saying to Cheyenne, "Mommy and daddy are going to hold you real soon". She spoke life to Cheyenne. After a while Kenisha went back to her room and laid down. She was hurting and in pain. The nurse brought her some more medicine and Kenisha was on cloud nine. The medicine made her drowsy and so she fell back to sleep and when she woke up she seen that David had been there in the room. The nurse came in to give Kenisha what she requested for dinner. Kenisha ate her food and got up to go see if David went down to visit Cheyenne while she was sleep. When she got down there she saw David talking to Cheyenne and holding her hand. Kenisha walked up on him and put her arms around his neck and gave him a kiss on the check. "Hey sweetheart", David said. I see that you are up. "Yes, I just finish eating too. I can't wait to get out of here to get some for real food cause this hospital food is a joke", Kenisha said. "You should have said something cause I would have brought you some food while I was on my way up here", David said. "I am glad you said that because when you come tomorrow bring me a gyro and you know how I like it", she said. "I can do that for you. Has the doctor said anything more to you about Cheyenne's condition", he said? "No he hasn't and I have been down here pretty much all day but you know what, he ain't got to say anything because I know that we will be taking her home soon", she said. "Did Rick and Tyenna come while I was at home", he asked? "Yeah they came up and you know Rick had jokes', he said. "I 'bout know he did. What did he say", David asked? "Just crackin' on my height and how the baby doesn't look like me", she said. "Oh they think she looks like me. That's why Rick is my boi", he said. "Whateva David! You know she looks like me", she said. "Okay sweetheart if you say so", he said while snickering. "Don't patronize me David", Kenisha said while laughing. "On the third day the doctor came in to see both Kenisha and David and said well we have been watching Cheyenne's breathing for a few days and she is fine. She is breathing like she should and you get to take her home tomorrow. They are taking the tubes out of her now and then they will bring her down to you soon after that okay". "Thank you sir. My wife and I appreciate it", David said. "Well Mr. Langley I am just glad that I could deliver you some good news", the doctor said. "We knew that God would bring her out. It is all Him", David said. The nurses brought down Cheyenne and they finally got to hold their first baby girl. They were so excited. They was thanking God and praising Him and giving Him all the glory.

Chapter 8
"Witnesses of God"

Then a man and a woman came and said, "excuse us but my name is Eddie and this is my wife Ivy". "Hello", David and Kenisha said. "Hi, how are you doing?" the couple said. "We are blessed," said David and Kenisha. "We don't mean to intrude but we have a son in NICU and he has the same problem with breathing just as your daughter had. We watched ya'll talk to your daughter and pray over her and now she gets to go home. She was only in there for three days and our son has been in there for about three weeks and we were wondering if you guys could pray over our son", Eddie said. "Well sir my name is David and this is my wife Kenisha. Is it alright if I ask you a question Eddie"? "Yeah sure David", he said. "Do you recognize Jesus Christ as your personal savior", David said? "We go to church", Eddie said. "That's awesome that you go to church. So how is your relationship with God", David said? "We pray and stuff and sing in the choir and my wife is over the youth department', Eddie said. "Let me ask you like this. Is your relationship with Christ the same or better than your relationship with your wife? Do you talk to Him just as much as you talk to your wife", David asked? "I don't understand what you mean", Eddie responded. "Well before we got married to our wives we were dating. We dated girls that we just considered to be cool or friends. We also dated girls that we couldn't trust, girls that we could date but couldn't bring home to momma, and then we dated one woman that we could make our wife. We made a commitment to them. Which level are you at? Have you asked God to come into your heart and confessed your sins to Him and believe that He died and rose again? Have you made a commitment to Him? Or have you went to church and haven't made a commitment unto God? Are you guys saved", David asked? "No sir we are not. Nobody ever asked us like that before", Eddie said. "I have no doubt that you guys love the Lord so what is stopping you from giving God your life", asked David? "We thought that going to church was good enough", Eddie replied. "Well going to church is good but let us kick some knowledge to you all that we learned in our evangelism class then afterwards that we can walk down and pray for your son. Is that all right", David said? "That will be cool. Whatcha got for us", Eddie said? "As stated in Ephesians chapter 2 verse 8-9, *for by grace are ye saved through faith; and that not of yourselves; it is the gift of God: 9 not of works, lest any man should boast.* See hear it is clear that it is not works that save us, not me, not you, not my wife, not your wife. It's God's grace. What will it mean to God if all we did was go to church and never let Him come into our heart and make our lives better and for Him to accomplish in us what He desires to do with us", David ministered? "I guess it wouldn't mean much if we just went to church and that was it", Eddie said. So everything that we have done up until now means nothing? "I don't mean to sound bold or harsh but that is exactly it because if you don't have God in your life then you are not living for Him you are living for yourself", said David. You love God right? "Yes we do", Eddie said. "So then why not give Him your life. He gave His son for you. According to John chapter 3 verse 16, *For God so loved the world, that He gave His only begotten Son, so that whosoever believeth in him shall not perish but have everlasting life.* That is how much God loves all of us. Jesus was born into this world, became an example for how we are to live, died and rose again with all power. Do ya'll know anyone that would go through what Jesus went through for you", David asked? "Man naw and I can't say that I would do the same for anybody else", Eddie said. "So you see it's more than just going to church and it's so many benefits for being in Christ. The bible is filled with God's promises if we would live our lives before Him in the manner and standards that He has set. Now don't get me wrong we all will go through trials and tribulations. No one is exempt from that which is called life because life can throw us some curve balls. So after hearing what God has already done for you, would you and your wife like to get saved", said David? "Yes," said Eddie. "What about you Ivy," asked Kenisha. "I don't know", Ivy said. "Do you have questions about what my husband said", Kenisha asked her? "Well yes I do", Ivy said in a confused tone. "Go ahead then. What are your questions", Kenisha asked confidently? "My first question is this: why would anyone let me be over the youth department if being saved is so important", she asked? "Ivy, I can't speak for anybody else but working in the church is just that working. You should be saved working in any auxiliary in a church. I am not sure what happened in your case. Maybe they thought that you were already saved and so they never asked. Who knows but it is only important that you know that according to Ephesians chapter 2 and verses 8-9 that works is not salvation and is also not what saves you. That's why my husband showed you in the bible exactly what the scripture said. Let me ask you this do you believe that salvation is important", Kenisha said? "Yes I do believe that it is important", Ivy said. "That is why God has brought you and your husband to us so that you guys can know Him and be brought into His fold. God loves you Ivy and that's why He doesn't want you to continue to deceive yourself. I believe that you are doing beautiful work in your church but if you would invite Jesus into your heart you will know the fullness of His Spirit in the name of our Lord and Savior Jesus Christ. Let me give you an example: let's say that you went grocery shopping and you came into my line to check out. I rang up all your food, took your money, and gave you your receipt, would you believe that I did my work", Kenisha implied? "Yes you did your job", Ivy said. "Okay, now here is the twist. I was never hired to work at that grocery store so knowing this do you think that store would pay me for the work that I did", Kenisha asked? "No they wouldn't", she said. "Why Ivy", Kenisha said? "Because they never hired you and so you are not on the payroll", she replied. "Ivy it's the same thing in the spiritual realm. You are working for God but not receiving the rewards or the benefits of knowing Him. Don't work for free. Let Jesus in and receive what He has for you. God has much in store for you but you first have to be hired into His kingdom", Kenisha said. "You know no one has ever put it to me like that before", Ivy said. "God knows how to relate to each of us. He knows how to reach all of us at our individual levels. Would you like to join your husband in salvation, Kenisha said"? "Yes Kenisha I would". Let's turn to Romans chapter 10 verse 9, say this with us, I, Eddie and Ivy *confess with my mouth the Lord Jesus, and I believe in my heart that God has raised him from the dead, I shall be saved.* Now repeat after me; Lord please forgive me for all my sins (Lord please forgive me for all my sins) knowingly and unknowingly in the name of Jesus (knowingly and unknowingly in the name of Jesus). David will pray now", said Kenisha. "Lord God we come to you rejoicing that two more souls have now been added to Your kingdom. We thank you for the ready hearts of your servants. We praise you for this couple. We ask that You would lead and guide them into all righteousness in the name of Jesus. We ask that You would continue to minister to their hearts and teach them your paths and write your commandments upon their hearts in the name of Jesus. Open up their understanding of your word even the more God in the name of Jesus. We ask for your covering for their marriage and their family. We ask for the healing of their son that is in NICU right now in the name of Jesus. Comfort them and take the pains and hurts away and let them believe by faith that their son is healed by the stripes of Jesus Christ in the name of our Lord and Savior. Let it be by your power and love that all situations be made right in their lives in the name of Jesus. We thank you and we praise you in Jesus name we pray. Amen". Eddie and Ivy cried unto the Lord and just thanked Him for His goodness and mercies. David said, "Here is my card with our phone number on it and this is the church that we go to if you ever decide that you want to visit". Please call us if you have any questions. Can we get your phone number so we can call and check up on you"? "Sure. Here are our names and phone number. We appreciate the word that you gave us", Eddie said. "Praise God," Kenisha said. "Are ya'll ready to walk down to NICU so we can pray over your son", David said? "Yeah, come on let's go", Ivy answered. David carried Cheyenne and they walked down to NICU and prayed over Eddie and Ivy's son Michael. David held the baby's hand and he prayed in a calm and soothing voice. He didn't call attention to himself or to others. You could hardly tell what was going on. Kenisha told Ivy to, "always remember that no matter what it looks like always speak positive". David and Kenisha said, "bye to the couple and told them that they will keep in touch and waiting to hear a good report about their baby boy Michael". Kenisha and

Cheyenne was released from the hospital the next day. They picked up their sons from Tyenna's house and went home.

Chapter 9
"Beginning of Ministry"

David and Kenisha was relaxing at home with their new daughter and enjoying her. Jabreel and Deon were excited about their new baby sister. They helped out around the house and with the baby. Saints from the church stopped by and called to see how everyone was doing. Kenisha healed from the c-section she had. Things around the house were getting back to normal and David went back to work. The boys were back in school from summer break. Now it's just Cheyenne and Kenisha at home. Kenisha is in her prayer closet praying unto God. She has set the atmosphere of worship.

"Lord God I bless you and I praise you. You are the Almighty God, the God of Abraham, of Isaac, of Jacob, and my God. You are my light, my hero, and my justifier. You God are the air that I breathe, my song, and my lullaby. How I love you God. No man will ever know how much I love you. You are the truth within me. You God are my instructor, my guide, and my teacher in the name of Jesus. I love you more than anyone would ever know. Lord I desire for you more than a little bit. How I long to abide in You and you in me in the name of Jesus. Lord I love you. You mean so much to me. There is no other who has my heart like you do. Please forgive me for all my sins knowingly and unknowingly in the name of Jesus. Lord God clean me up on the inside. Whatever is not like you that is in me I ask that you take it out of me right now in the name of Jesus. I want to be blameless at your return. I seek to be apart of the church that is without spot or wrinkle. Lord God I just desire to be pleasing in your sight in the name of Jesus. In all that I do I desire to please you. I seek to line up with your word, your instructions, and the example that you have set for me in the name of Jesus. I desire to serve you with everything that is within me. Father in the name of Jesus please bring to my remembrance any fault or any offence that I may have caused that I may get it right with you and my brother or sister in the Lord. God I just hold you near and dear to my heart. How I love thee in the name of Jesus. I seek to be a child of obedience. Obedient to your word and towards your people saved and unsaved in the name of Jesus. I realize now that it is obedience that pleases you more than anything else. Through obedience Lord is liberty in the name of Jesus. My Father, I seek to be all that you have purposed for me to be. Lord I lift up my husband to you in the name of Jesus. I put him in your hands oh God. I declare that he is that awesome man of God that you have called for him to be in the name of Jesus. I declare that he is a man after your own heart in the name of Jesus. I declare that he is a just and faithful man in the name of Jesus. I declare that he is a loyal man of God in the name of Jesus. I declare that when he speaks he speaks with power behind his words in the name of Jesus. I declare that my husband is a man of obedience in Christ in the name of Jesus. I bind the hand of the enemy that would desire to destroy my husband in the name of Jesus. Father your Spirit is dominate in my husband. I lift up my children unto you. I declare that our children are praisers and worshippers of God in the name of Jesus. I declare that our children are witnesses of You, declaring Your goodness in the streets in the name of Jesus. I pray for my children's spouses that you have set for them. I ask that our children's spouse love You and serve You in the name of Jesus. I also pray that they love each other, as a married couple should in the name of Jesus. Bless them to be faithful unto You. Lord I pray that they all stay pure until marriage in the name of Jesus. Don't allow them to be sucked in and deceived into the wrong crowd in the name of Jesus. Lord God teach us as parents in how to direct and correct our children. Lead us in how to encourage them when harm comes to them. We seek to train them in the correct manner Father with your help in the name of Jesus. Cover and protect them especially when we are not around in the name of Jesus. Let our children know you for themselves. Lord God be real to them in the name of Jesus. I declare that this house is a house of prayer in the name of Jesus. I declare and desire that when people come into our house that it be a house of peace, a house of restoration, a house of healing, a house of deliverance, and a house of freedom in the name of Jesus. It is all about a soul hallelujah. Any spirit that tries to enter this home that is not like You will be checked at the door in the name of Jesus. Your word says that *if we submit to God, resist the devil, then he will flee from us.* We dedicate our home to You for You to do as You see fit in the name of Jesus. Nothing but Your Spirit will dwell in this place. I plead the blood of Jesus over my family. I plead the blood of Jesus over our ministries collectively as a family, our five areas of ministries, which is our soul, spirit, body, finances, and our social areas in the name of Jesus and also our individual ministries. I plead the blood of Jesus over our home, our vehicles and please keep us safe from car accidents and any other accidents that there can be in the name of Jesus. I plead the blood of Jesus over our careers and our businesses. I plead the blood of Jesus over our children's learning education and school. I plead the blood of Jesus over our minds and hearts. Lord God I love You and I just enjoy being in your presence. I thank you for Your Spirit in the name of Jesus I pray. I ask that You would lead my family and me in all righteousness on today.

Lead us and guide us by your Spirit in the name of Jesus. Lord God bless us to be a blessing on today in the name of Jesus. Lead us to a soul on today. Lord we bless your name…. "Waaaah, waaah, waaah….", Cheyenne cried. "Oh Lord Cheyenne is crying. I bless your name in Jesus name I pray this prayer. Amen", Kenisha said.

"Come on baby girl. Are you hungry? Let mommy get you some milk. I got to feed tha baby don't I", she said. Kenisha feed Cheyenne and changed her and then put her to sleep. They took a nap and Kenisha woke up in time to get her boys off the school bus. She cooked dinner and went over the boy's homework with them. Then David came home from work. "Hey Sweet", said David. "Hey Baby how was work", Kenisha said. "Work was all right", sighed David. "What, did one of your soldiers do something again", Kenisha asked? "Naw actually they were straight. It was really just being in that heat all day. That heat was no joke", David said. "I bet. Cheyenne and I was in tha air condition all day. It was real cool", she said. "Ha ha"! That's all right. I see you got jokes", David said. "Yeah well I ain't pregnant no more so it's back on til tha break of dawn", she said. "That's all right though Kenisha. Let me go upstairs and get out of this monkey suit", he said. "Okay, dinner will be ready soon", she said. "All right I will be down after I finish getting myself together", he said. After David was finished he came downstairs and the family ate together. They had family night. Jabreel wanted to go bowling so that's where the family went, to the bowling alley. They had a good time too. Everyone really enjoyed them selves.

The next morning the phone rang. "Hello", said Kenisha. "Hello. May I speak to Kenisha please?" "This is she. Who's calling, said Kenisha? "It's Ivy. You know the one from the hospital", she said. "Oh hey how are you doing", Kenisha said? "I'm good", Ivy said. "What have you been up to", Kenisha asked? "Nothing much but taking care of my baby boy Michael", Ivy explained. "My goodness ya'll must be at home", Kenisha said. "Yes we are and we are so excited. We brought Michael home about 3 weeks ago", she said with excitement. "Really! That's awesome! God is good isn't He", Kenisha said? "Yes He is. My husband Eddie and I really appreciate you and your husband. We didn't get to leave the hospital as soon as we had liked but nevertheless, we got to bring home our son. Eddie and I just really wanted to thank you guys for your prayers", she said. "Ivy that's all God and He alone gets the glory. We are just vessels for His use. I am glad we could be apart of it. How are you doing with your relationship with God", Kenisha asked? "You know what I have never felt so alive in all my life. God has really given me true happiness. I have been out telling everyone about God and salvation. I have never done that before", Ivy said. "Do you know why you can do that now; it's because of God's spirit that has been birthed into you. He has given you His spirit. Are there any questions that you have", Kenisha asked further? "Not right now. I am reading the bible more and praying more and God is revealing so much to me. I have never experienced Him like this before. I wanted to come visit your church this Sunday. I was hoping that we could follow you guys to your church", Ivy said. "Are you and your husband in agreement about visiting our church", Kenisha enquired? "Oh yes. We have been trying to find the church but we could never find it and that's why I was calling to see if we could follow you", she said. "Yeah sure ya'll may follow us. Where do you live", Kenisha said? "We stay on post", she said. "So do we Ivy, which subdivision", she said? "We stay in Weaven Village by gate 3", Ivy said. "Okay, we are in New Weaven. This is so awesome that we live so close to each other. I know that this is God appointed, boy!" Kenisha said with excitement. "We go to Sunday School so we usually leave here by 8:30 a.m. so we can get a seat. So how about we meet at Gate 3 shoppette", she said. "That's cool Kenisha", she said. "We will be in the silver Denali Ivy", she said. "Okay then we will see you Sunday then Kenisha", she said. "Cool, Ivy we look forward to it", she said. "Bye Kenisha", said Ivy. "Bye", said she told Ivy. "God you are so awesome"! Kenisha yelled out loud. She yelled so loud she scared Cheyenne and woke her up. "Oh baby mommy is so sorry. Cheyenne, I have gots to call your daddy and tell him this. Kenisha got on the phone and called David and said, "baby I just had to call you. Remember that couple that we ministered to in the hospital", Kenisha said? "Yeah, what about them', said David? "She just called me and she was saying how she had never experienced God like this before and they are going to follow us to church on Sunday", she said. "Man that's awesome! God is truly doing His thang", David said. "I know right. Well we are going to have to make sure that we are on time. So you know what that means, you are going to have to get up so forget about any extra sleep", Kenisha said. "I may sleep over just because you said that Kenisha", he said. "I trust that you will make the right decision because you are an awesome man of God", she said. David just smiled and laughed and said, "man I hate when you do that". "I knowwww", Kenisha said laughing. "Well hey Sweet I have to go back to work now so I will see you when I get home from work okay", he said. "Okay Babe, I love you. Bye", she said. "I love you too Sweet. Bye", he said.

Kenisha went in her prayer closet like she does every morning. While she was in prayer Kenisha had a vision. She saw herself at a shelter for teens and women. She saw herself teaching the word of God. She also saw teenagers and women crying, repenting, releasing, being healed, and giving their lives to God. When she came out of the vision Kenisha began to just weep and cry out to God praising Him and thanking Him for His goodness. Kenisha began to speak with tongues as the spirit gave utterance. After she came out of prayer she started studying the bible. Kenisha got herself and Cheyenne dressed and they went to the store and while she was there she ran into someone that she knew. "Hey Shemila! What is going on with you", Kenisha said. "Girl nothing much but tryin' to deal with this deployment", Shemila said. "Oh Derrick is in Iraq", Kenisha asked? "Yes girl and it is so hard for me. I don't know what to do with myself. I try to stay busy and keep the children encouraged but I ain't gone even lie it is a task. How did you do it when David went to Iraq", Shemila asked? "First and foremost I couldn't have done it without God. He is the only reason that I made it through because I if I didn't have him I wouldn't have made it. I missed my husband dearly and the boys, maaan they drove me up one wall and down another", she said. "Kenisha I know what you mean", she said. "However, check this out Shemila, God is who helped me. He led me and guided me throughout the whole deployment. Some days were better than others but nevertheless it was God who got me through. He also sent people my way to help me out with the boys and I was so ever grateful. Do you go to church", she asked? "No I don't. Kenisha the church is full of hypocrites and I ain't got time for all the drama. I have enough drama in my life", Shemila responded. "I will say that there are some people who don't walk the life of a Christian as they should but that shouldn't depict how you should live your life now does it? If you know what a Christian should behave like then why not be the one to be that example that someone else may need.

It is so easy to point the finger at others and I am not going to even say that those type people aren't saved because God's word says that, *being confident of this, that he who has began a good work in you will carry it on to completion until the day of Jesus Christ. (Philippians 1:6 NIV)* There is also another scripture that says, *we have all sinned and fallen short of the glory of God. (Romans 3:23a NIV)* We are all a work in progress. I have sinned. You have sinned. We all have sinned. There is no one on this earth that has not sinned", she said. "I hear what you are saying Kenisha but the fact still remains that as a "supposed to be Christian" you all are to set a standard. No one expects a Christian attitude from an unsaved person", Shemila said. "Let me ask you this then Shemila. You know that I am saved right", Kenisha asked? "Yeah I know that", she answered. "Do you refer to me as a hypocrite", Kenisha questioned? "No as far as I know you live what you say", she replied. "See you classified all Christians earlier as hypocrites and yet here I am and you just said that you didn't feel that I was a hypocrite so doesn't that count for something? Now before you answer that think about it like this: you know how some people stereotype all black people the same because of the actions of a few", Kenisha asked. "Yeah", she answered. "Now doesn't that make you upset because you don't fall into some people's typical category of black people", Kenisha said. "Yeah that does make me upset", she said. "So tell me then Shemila why does that make you upset", Kenisha enquired? "Because I don't do what others "*claim*" that black people do", she said. "That's what I am talking about. It has absolutely nothing to do with stereotypes because some people of all races do all things that are immoral but some races are more publicized than others. The important thing is, do you see where I am coming from", Kenisha said. "Yeah I get the point", Shemila said. "I encourage you to come and visit my church and meet Jesus Christ", she said. "You ain't in no cult are you Kenisha", Shemila said? "Naw girl I ain't in no cult wit yo' silly self. What I mean by that is if you come and visit there will be a word for you and the only way to get to the Father is to go through His Son Jesus Christ. I tell you that you will know a peace, as you never have known before. If you want to know how I made it through the Iraq deployment come to church and you will know because the only thing that I can tell you is that God did it, He lead me, He guided me, He loved me, He comforted me in my lonely times, He wiped the tears from my eyes when I missed my husband the most. He even gave me peace with the children. It was all God and there was nothing in particular that I did. I never thought that I could handle my husband being gone for so long, coming home, then leaving again within a year. But God said that He would never leave us nor forsake us and He kept His word. If you have never met a person that keeps their word then meet God because He always does. Here is my card with my phone number on it and the times that we are in church. As a matter of fact we have bible study tomorrow at 7:00 and you are welcome to come. The directions for the church are on the back of the card. I hope to see you there", Kenisha said with expectancy. "I won't be there at bible study and I will think about coming to church on Sunday", Shemila boldly said. "Well I am not going to push you but I will ask you this: would you like to make Jesus Christ your Lord and Savior today? He loves you and cares about you and He wants you to make Him apart of your life all you have to do is invite Him in", she said. "I'm really not ready Kenisha", she said. "Okay but I am going to keep checking up on you and inviting you so you are going to have to give in sooner or later. I love you and if you need anything please don't hesitate to call. If you want some time for yourself then let me know and I will watch the babies for you. Even if you just want company or to talk give me a ring or stop by", she said. "Thank you Kenisha. I really appreciate that. I will keep that in mind", she said. "Well Shemila I have got to go before my little one wakes up before I finish shopping. You know how that can go", Kenisha said. "Yeah girl I know. It was sure good seeing you Kenisha. I will see you around. Bye", she said. "I know that you will Shemila. Bye girl", she said.

    Kenisha finished her shopping and went home. She told David about her day and he told her about his day. Sunday's and bible studies came and went and their was no Shemila. Kenisha just kept her in her prayers and called her once in a while to encourage her to come to church and see if she needed anything. She also continued to pray, as we all should continue to pray for someone that we've witnessed to. Sometimes when we witness they don't accept Christ right away or even come to church but continue to pray for them and invite them to Christ and watch the love of God manifest.

Chapter 10
"Ministry Doesn't Stop"

One day it was pretty outside. It wasn't too hot or too cold so Kenisha went walking with Cheyenne in the stroller and found herself at a park. She just chilled and relaxed on the park bench and watched Cheyenne smile and laugh at the other children in the park. Then a lady came and sat by Kenisha and started talking to her. "It is a wonderful day isn't it", said the lady. "Yes it is pretty nice", said Kenisha. "How old is baby", the lady said. "She is 4 months", Kenisha said. "She is so cute and she looks like a little baby doll", the lady said. "Thank you. How old are your children", Kenisha said. "My son is 2 years old and my daughter is 4 years old", said the lady. "Do you stay here on post", Kenisha asked? "Yes said the lady but I don't know for how long though". "Oh are you all moving to another post", Kenisha said? "No, I haven't made up my mind if I want to stay married to my husband", the lady said. "Why do you say that if you don't mind my asking? What has brought you to this conclusion", she asked inquisitively? "Ever since my husband came back from Iraq he hasn't been the same. I think he is having a hard time readjusting from Iraq and I can't deal with it anymore", the lady sadly said. "Let me ask you this: Is he cheating on you", she said? "No, at least I don't believe so. There aren't any signs", said the lady. "Is he a good father to your children", she asked? "Yes he is. It is not any of those things it's just that he is so distant. He won't talk to me about anything but I am the one who takes all the crap", said the lady. "Let me introduce myself before we move forward into this conversation. My name is Kenisha and your name is", she said? "My name is Sarah", she said. "It's nice to meet you Sarah", she said. "Nice to meet you too Kenisha", she said. "Do you all have a church home", Kenisha said? "Yes we go to church sometimes but we aren't members of one. We haven't found the right church yet. My home church is in Arizona", said Sarah. "Do you have a relationship with Jesus Christ", Kenisha asked? "Yes. I pray all the time. I read my bible everyday and pray for understanding", she said. "That is awesome Sarah. That's real good. Well let me encourage you then with the word of God. You really have no reason to leave your husband. You all are just going through a rough patch right now and God will get you through it. Don't you want to see God in all His glory in your marriage", she said? "Yes that would be just great Kenisha but I have been going through this for so long that I don't think that I will see God in all His glory in my marriage", she said. "You know Sarah God can do ALL things but fail. The bible is filled with God's promises and being healed in your marriage is one of them. My God, our God is all what we need for Him to be. He is the great I Am and there is no other who can do what He can and you have to know that. Are you and your husband in counseling", Kenisha asked? "No. He won't go because he says that he doesn't need counseling. I have tried everything….", Sarah said. "But have you tried God", Kenisha suggested. "I thought I did", she said. "Sarah let me tell you something if you try God and believe in faith He will perform a miracle in your marriage but not only in that but also in your heart and in your husband's heart you have to only believe. You just have to have faith. God can only operate in faith. Read Hebrews chapter 11 and you will see that God is pleased when we His people walk in faith", she said. Sarah's eyes began to fill with tears. "Let God be the glue in your marriage. If you fall in love with God even the more, you will see changes in your marriage.

It's all about intimacy. Become intimate with God and be lead by Him. Look up scriptures concerning marriage in the bible and repeat them daily until it gets into your spirit and becomes alive in you. I want to invite you to come and visit my church. Here is my card and it has all my information on it. My pastor is Pastor Rural and I believe that he can help you guys. Come on Sunday and I will introduce you and your husband to my pastor and co-pastor. They are a man and woman of God that is truly led by the Spirit of God and they are down to earth people that are serious about souls for Christ. They are examples to follow and in all that they do they live by the wisdom of God and I know that they can help you. I really hope to see you there and I will be looking for you", she said. "Thank you so much Kenisha. I really needed to hear that", Sarah said. "God knows what we need at all times and this is just proof that He wants to do something radical in your marriage", she said. "Thank you Kenisha but I have to be going now so I can fix the children's lunch", she said. "It was nice meeting you Sarah and like I said I will be looking forward to seeing you Sunday", she said. "I will be there", Sarah said with enthusiasm! "See you then. Bye Sarah", Kenisha said. "Come on Matt and Brittany. Let's head home so we can eat lunch", Sarah said. "Okay mommy," said the children.

Sarah and her family came that following Sunday and they truly enjoyed service. Her husband gave his life to the Lord. The sermon was off tha chain that Sunday. God pricked the heart of His people that day. Kenisha introduced them to Pastor and Co-Pastor Rural. The family joined the church after visiting the church for about 2 months and because faith was a factor and totally gave themselves over to God, their marriage was healed. It's all about reaching a soul. Leading them to Christ so that He can do the rest. In order for someone to become saved and make the confession of Christ's birth, death, and resurrection, they have to be told by someone who knows and believes in Christ.

    Kenisha is sitting on her swing on the porch, swinging back and forth and relaxing while Cheyenne is taking a nap. She heard her neighbor Tamara crying on the phone. Kenisha waited for her to get off the phone before she went over. She started praying for her neighbor and that God would give her what to say and lead her in what to do. All God told Kenisha to do "was to be a comfort to her because Tamara was hurting and she is angry with Him". After Tamara got off the phone Kenisha went over there and asked her if she was okay. Tamara just cried and said, "I don't understand why God would let this happen", Kenisha's neighbor said. "What's wrong Tamara", Kenisha asked her? "I found out that my father died", Tamara said. "I am so sorry to hear that. Is there anything that I can do", Kenisha said? "No. I don't think there is anything that anyone can do for me right now", Tamara said. "I will be praying for you and your family", Kenisha said calmly. Then Tamara yelled, "I am so angry at God". "You know Tamara I have never lost a parent so I can't say that I understand what you are going through but I do know about losing someone whom you love so dear. I do know that it does hurt and all kinds of things run through your mind. Your mind is going non-stop. I know it hurts and I also know that with time wounds heal. God does heal and comfort you. When losing someone that is dear to me I try not to wonder why but I do. I don't think that there is a reason that I would accept even if He told it to me. I want you to know that I love you and God loves you too. Don't shut Him out at a time like this. Keep an open mind. I am here for you. When do you leave to go home", Kenisha said? "I am leaving first thing in the morning", said Tamara. "Is there anything that you need for me to do while you are out of town", she said? "Actually if you can check my mail for me and water my plants I would really appreciate it", said Tamara. "Okay it's done. Is there anything else", she said? No Kenisha thank you. That's all I need right now. I'm going to go back in the house and get myself ready to leave in the morning", Tamara said. "Can I pray with you before you go", Kenisha asked? "That's fine", Tamara said. "Lord God I am asking that you would bring comfort to Tamara and her family in this time of grievance in the name of Jesus. All we desire is for Your will to be done. I ask that you would give them safe traveling grace there and back in the name of Jesus. Bless the hearts to be receptive when the word comes at the funeral. Open the ears to hear and bring sight to the eyes and open the hearts to receive Your word in the name of Jesus. Turn anger into joy and frustration into peace in the name of Jesus. Lord God we bless You and we love You in Jesus name we pray. Amen", she prayed. Kenisha left and went into the house and Tamara went in and finished packing so that she and her family could leave in the morning. Kenisha just continued to keep Tamara in her prayers.

After a family dinner, David and Kenisha were spending quality time together the phone rang. "Hello," David said. "Hey David this is Naomi is Kenisha there?" "Yeah here she is," David said. "Hello," Kenisha said. "Hey Kenisha this is Naomi", she said. "Oh hey Naomi what's up", she said? "Going through girl and I just need someone to talk to", she said. "Why, what's up Naomi", she asked? Naomi went on to explain what was going on and said, "I can't find a job and what the military is paying Kip ain't cuttin' it. We got bills out tha ying yang and I am at my wits end. We don't have enough food to last us til next payday. Shoot I don't even know if we have enough food til the end of the week. Girl I have prayed and prayed and prayed for a turn around in our finances and I am coming up empty handed". "Hey Naomi hold on for just a second, al'ight", Kenisha said. "Al'ight", Naomi responded. Kenisha put her on hold and told David, "Kip and Naomi needs food is it was okay if we help them". David said, "Yeah most definitely that's cool". Kenisha got back on the phone and said, "Hey Naomi I am back. I just talked to David and we will bring you guys some groceries tomorrow morning unless ya'll need it tonight". "Naw we don't need it tonight", she said. "Naomi what are you all in need of", she asked? "Whatever you bless us with will be fine", she responded. "No, that will not be fine. The bible says *you have not because you ask not* so if you don't tell us what you need then we won't know", she boldly stated. "We need some meat, breakfast food, and some lunch food", said Naomi. "Have you called Pastor about your financial situation", Kenisha asked? "No, I don't want to let them know what is going on. I can't let them know what I am going through", Naomi said. "There is no need to be embarrassed. We had to do the same thing at one time and one thing you need to know is that pride won't get you fed and your bills paid but there is a lesson to be learned in all of this. We have to be good stewards of what God has given us. I am here to help but I can't be counseling you that is for Pastor Rural to do. If you don't say anything to him, he can't help. Then the blood will be on my hands if something bad happens and I have had information about your status and didn't say or do anything. I will have to let pastor know. I won't give details but I will have to let him know that you guys are in need of help and that you all will need some counseling. He is the pastor and he can do more than I can. All I can do is encourage you and tell you that God can because I know that for myself. Just believe and trust in Him and things will get better for you. There is a job that God has for you but you have to continue to get out there and put in applications and keep the faith. Now, I can tell you this though, find some scriptures concerning finances and repeat them daily until you believe it for yourself. Pronounce the blessings on your household, your life, your family, your husband, your finances and whatever else. David and I will be over at about 11:00. Is that alright with you", Kenisha said? "Yeah that is fine. We will pay you guys back", Naomi said. "No it's not about that. Just receive the blessing. You don't owe us anything. God is whom you give the glory to. We don't want anything in return. Talk to Pastor Rural please", she pleaded. "We will talk to him. As a matter of fact, we will call him tomorrow", she said. "Thank you Naomi and you will see that it will all work out", she said. "Again, thank you Kenisha and tell David we thank him as well", she said. "All right Naomi we will see you guys tomorrow okay", she said. "Cool, I will talk to you tomorrow Kenisha, bye", she said. "Bye Naomi", she said.

    David and Kenisha finished spending their quality time together and took the phone off the hook. Even though we minister we have to know that our ministry starts at home first. That is how we keep our Jerusalem straight. The only way we can be effective outside of the home is if our home is being ministered to on a daily basis. There is a balance in it all and that's one thing that God wants us to have more than anything is balance. If we don't have balance we are unstable somewhere and being unstable is not pleasing to God. Think of it like this, say you have a broken leg, you are unstable physically and you need crutches to get around. Without the crutches it is a 90% chance that you are going to fall. It's the same in the spirit realm. We have to have a balance or something will go lacking.

    Kenisha is still fulfilling all that God is purposing for her to do in life. The main thing is that she had to become free before she could fully walk in God's purpose for her life. Her visions came to pass and are still coming to pass. She ministers at shelters, speaks to teenage girls and women, teaching encouragement, how to be happy with yourself, always letting them know that you can never fill someone else's shoes. God has shoes made only for you and those are for you to fill. Kenisha's heart is to let young ladies and women know that they are worth a whole lot more to God than what they believe. She let's them know who they are in Christ and that He came down to take their place. Her desire is for women to realize that it's not about them and it never was. It's all about a soul and if we never went through anything then we can't minister to someone else that is hurting. The best way to get over something is to take the focus off of yourself and minister to the soul that is in bondage. She travels and ministers all over the world. She draws with her testimonies, with the love of God and faith in knowing that God is ALL IN ALL. Kenisha has seen young ladies and women being delivered, set free, restored, healed, and giving their lives to the Jesus Christ. That is her prayer and her prayers are being fulfilled.

LET FREEDOM REIGN IN YOU

Kenisha found freedom and so can you, give it to God, I Peter 5:7 KJV says, *casting all your care on Him; for He careth for you.* Kenisha isn't just a character; she has a real life name. Her name could be yours or it could be mine, whatever is the trial or trials that we go through as women, God is yet in control of it all and there is freedom, there is closure and after closure there is life. There is no more bondage unless you decide to become entangled with it again. Galatians 5:1 NIV says, *"It is for freedom that Christ has set us free. Stand firm, then, and do not let yourselves be burdened again by a yoke of slavery.* You can stay free. You are somebody in Christ. I Peter 2:9 NIV says, *"but you are a chosen people, a royal priesthood, a holy nation, a people belonging to God, that you may declare the praises of him who called you out of darkness into his wonderful light."* We are royalty. We are queens and princesses. Never let anyone tell you different not even your circumstances. Nothing and no one dictates who you are in God because He has already said in His word who you are. Know it. Believe it and live by it. God is tugging on your heart, *he that has an ear let him hear what the spirit is saying,* when God is knocking on your door harden not your heart, there is deliverance. You can let the things of this world knock you down or you can stand on the Word of God and take the world by storm. Your freedom is up to you. If you desire to be free just pray what is in your heart because the best way to be free is what you confess to, admit to, and be truthful with God. I can't write a prayer for that because only you know what is in your heart. Give Him your heart and you will begin to know true freedom. I really can't explain freedom because it's not something that

I can explain. All I can say is that it feels so good to truly be me. If you desire salvation say this scripture Romans 10:9 KJV, *I (put your name) confess with my mouth the Lord Jesus, and I (put your name) believe in my heart that God raised him from the dead, I (put your name) am saved* and then pray. God please forgive me for all of my sins. I repent and turn my life over to you. Teach me your paths and write your commandments on my heart. Turn my heart of stone into a heart of flesh in the name of Jesus. Thank you Jesus for going to the cross for me. I love you and I invite you into my heart to do as you please in Jesus name. Amen. If you said this prayer please find a good word church. Don't be burdened down by doctrine just do what the bible says. You now have God's Spirit and He will keep you while you find a good word church. Be lead by Him and He won't stir you wrong. (Remember to write down your spiritual birthday at the beginning of the book.) Please know that it's not about you but it's about how you can help someone else just like I am prayerfully helping you. You are not the only one who went through these things and maybe you haven't been through it but know someone who has, wouldn't it be awesome to help them get free? Be free in Jesus name and remember, to get to God you have to get past you. Amen.

Dunamis Publishing Co., LLC

Address: P.O. Box 2375, Ft. Campbell, KY. 42223

Email address: dunamispublishing@hotmail.com

More books are coming in 2007!

Visit Keisha on her website: www.msnusers.com/WordofPower. This website is used solely for the use of encouragement, salvation, prayer, praise, devotions, and etc. Come and be uplifted. Join in and be apart. Be blessed and ever increasing in Christ.